Practice*Planners*®

Arthur E. Jongsma, Jr., Series Editor

Helping therapists help their clients...

D1220624

PracticePlanners

Second Edition

THE COMPLETE ADULT
PSYCHOTHERAPY
Treatment Planner

A new, fully revised edition of the bestselling *The Complete
Psychotherapy Treatment Planner*, this invaluable resource features:

* Treatment plan components for 39
behaviorally based problems—including five
completely new problem sets

* A step-by-step guide to writing treatment plans

* Over 500 additional prewritten treatment goals,
objectives, and interventions

* Handy workbook format with space to record
your own treatment plan options

* Over 100,000 **Practice***Planners* sold

Arthur E. Jongsma, Jr., and L. Mark Peterson

PracticePlanners

Arthur E. Jongsma, Jr., Series Editor

Brief Therapy
**HOMEWORK
PLANNER**

*brief therapy
homework used to facilit*

* Contains 62 ready-to-copy homework assignments
that can be used to facilitate brief individual therapy

* Homework assignments and exercises are keyed to
over 30 behaviorally-based presenting problems from
The Complete Psychotherapy Treatment Planner

* Assignments may be quickly customized using the
enclosed disk

* Over 100,000 **Practice***Planners* sold

Includes disk

Gary M. Schultheis

PracticePlanners®

The Clinical
**DOCUMENTATION
SOURCEBOOK**

Second Edition

A Comprehensive Collection of
Mental Health Practice
Forms, Handouts, and Records

FEATURES

* Contains ready-to-use forms for managing
the mental health treatment process
* Covers every stage of the treatment process
* Includes customizable forms on disk
* Over 100,000 **Practice***Planners* sold

Includes Disk

Donald E. Wiger

PracticePlanners

Arthur E. Jongsma, Jr., Series Editor

**The Adult Psychotherapy
PROGRESS NOTES PLANNER**

This time-saving resource:

* Contains Progress notes components for the
behaviorally based problems

* Covers the gamut of possible outcomes for every
intervention suggested in the best-selling *Complete
Adult Psychotherapy Treatment Planner, 2nd Edition*

* Includes 1,000s of pre-written sessions and patient
presentation descriptions

* Provides a handy workbook format with space to
record your own progress note options

* Over 150,000 **Practice***Planners* sold

Arthur E. Jongsma, Jr.

Practice*Planners*®   Order Form

Treatment Planners cover all the necessary elements for developing formal treatment plans, including detailed problem definitions, long-term goals, short-term objectives, therapeutic interventions, and DSM-IV diagnoses.

Documentation Sourcebooks provide a comprehensive collection of ready-to-use blank forms, handouts, and questionnaires to help you manage your client reports and streamline the record keeping and treatment process. Features clear, concise explanations of the purpose of each form—including when it should be used and at what point. Includes customizable forms on disk.

The Complete Adult Psychotherapy Treatment Planner, Second Edition
0-471-31924-4 / $44.95

The Child Psychotherapy Treatment Planner, Second Edition
0-471-34764-7 / $44.95

The Adolescent Psychotherapy Treatment Planner, Second Edition
0-471-34766-3 / $44.95

The Chemical Dependence Treatment Planner
0-471-23795-7 / $44.95

The Continuum of Care Treatment Planner
0-471-19568-5 / $44.95

The Couples Psychotherapy Treatment Planner
0-471-24711-1 / $44.95

The Employee Assistance (EAP) Treatment Planner
0-471-24709-X / $44.95

The Pastoral Counseling Treatment Planner
0-471-25416-9 / $44.95

The Older Adult Psychotherapy Treatment Planner
0-471-29574-4 / $44.95

The Behavioral Medicine Treatment Planner
0-471-31923-6 / $44.95

The Group Therapy Treatment Planner
0-471-37449-0 / $44.95

The Family Therapy Treatment Planner
0-471-34768-X / $44.95

The Severe and Persistent Mental Illness Treatment Planner
0-471-35945-9 / $44.95

The Gay and Lesbian Psychotherapy Treatment Planner
0-471-35080-X / $44.95

The Clinical Documentation Sourcebook, Second Edition
0-471-32692-5 / $49.95

The Psychotherapy Documentation Primer
0-471-28990-6 / $45.00

The Couple and Family Clinical Documentation Sourcebook
0-471-25234-4 / $49.95

The Clinical Child Documentation Sourcebook
0-471-29111-0 / $49.95

The Chemical Dependence Treatment Documentation Sourcebook
0-471-31285-1 / $49.95

The Forensic Documentation Sourcebook
0-471-25459-2 / $85.00

The Continuum of Care Clinical Documentation Sourcebook
0-471-34581-4 / $75.00

NEW AND FORTHCOMING

The Traumatic Events Treatment Planner
0-471-39587-0 / $44.95

The Special Education Treatment Planner
0-471-38873-4 / $44.95 p

The Mental Retardation and Developmental Disability Treatment Planner
0-471-38253-1 / $44.95

The Social Work and Human Services Treatment Planner
0-471-37741-4 / $44.95

The Rehabilitation Psychology Treatment Planner
0-471-35178-4 / $44.95

Name_____

Affiliation_____

Address_____

City/State/Zip_____

Phone/Fax_____

E-mail_____

To order, call 1-800-753-0655
(Please refer to promo #1-4019 when ordering.)
Or send this page with payment* to:
John Wiley & Sons, Inc., Attn: J. Knott
605 Third Avenue, New York, NY 10158-0012

❏ Check enclosed   ❏ Visa   ❏ MasterCard   ❏ American Express

Card #_____

Expiration Date_____

Signature_____

*Please add your local sales tax to all orders.

www.wiley.com/practiceplanners

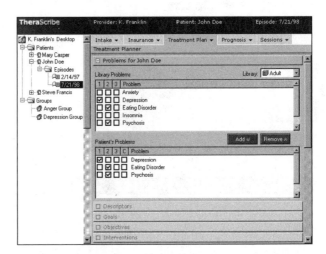

Brief Family Therapy
Homework Planner

Practice *Planners*®

Arthur E. Jongsma, Jr., Series Editor

Brief Family Therapy
Homework Planner

Louis J. Bevilacqua

Frank M. Dattilio

JOHN WILEY & SONS, INC.

New York • Chichester • Weinheim • Brisbane • Singapore • Toronto

This book is dedicated to our spouses Debbie Bevilacqua and Maryann Dattilio, and children Rachael, Amanda, and Lindsey Bevilacqua and Roseanne, Tara, and Michael Dattilio, who taught us the most of what we need to know about families.

Note about Photocopy Rights

The publisher grants purchasers permission to reproduce handouts from this book for professional use with their clients.

Library of Congress Cataloging-in-Publication Data:

Bevilacqua, Louis.
    Brief family therapy homework planner / Louis J. Bevilacqua, Frank M. Dattilio.
      p. cm.
    ISBN 0-471-38512-3 (pbk./disk : alk. paper)
      1. Family psychotherapy—Problems, exercises, etc.   2. Brief psychotherapy—Problems, exercises, etc.   3. Mental illness—Treatment.   I. Dattilio, Frank M.   II. Title.

RC488.5 .B493 2001
616.89'156—dc21   00-066253

Printed in the United States of America.

10 9 8 7 6 5 4 3 2 1

CONTENTS

PRACTICE PLANNER SERIES PREFACE

The practice of psychotherapy has a dimension that did not exist 30, 20, or even 15 years ago—accountability. Treatment programs, public agencies, clinics, and even group and solo practitioners must now justify the treatment of patients to outside review entities that control the payment of fees. This development has resulted in an explosion of paperwork.

Clinicians must now document what has been done in treatment, what is planned for the future, and what the anticipated outcomes of the interventions are. The books and software in this Practice Planner series are designed to help practitioners fulfill these documentation requirements efficiently and professionally.

The Practice Planner series is growing rapidly. It now includes not only the original *Complete Psychotherapy Treatment Planner* and *The Child and Adolescent Psychotherapy Treatment Planner*, but also *Treatment Planners* targeted to specialty areas of practice, including: chemical dependency, the continuum of care, couples therapy, family therapy, older adult treatment, employee assistance, behavioral medicine, pastoral counseling, and more.

In addition to the *Treatment Planners*, the series also includes *TheraScribe®: The Computerized Assistant to Psychotherapy Treatment Planning*, as well as adjunctive books, such as the *Brief Therapy, Chemical Dependence, Couples, Family*, and *Child Homework Planners, The Psychotherapy Documentation Primer*, and *Clinical, Forensic, Child, Couples and Family*, and *Chemical Dependence Documentation Sourcebooks*—containing forms and resources to aid in mental health practice management. The goal of the series is to provide practitioners with the resources they need in order to provide high-quality care in the era of accountability—or, to put it simply, we seek to help you spend more time on patients, and less on paperwork.

ARTHUR E. JONGSMA, JR.
Grand Rapids, Michigan

PREFACE

More and more therapists are assigning homework to their clients. Not only have short-term therapy models endorsed this practice, but the benefits are being recognized by many traditional therapists as well.

WHY HOMEWORK?

Assigning homework to psychotherapy clients is beneficial for several reasons. One important reason is due to the advent of managed care, which often requires shorter and fewer treatment sessions. To help maximize the effectiveness of briefer treatment under this system, therapists can assign between-session homework, which acts as an extension of the treatment process, as well as providing continuity and allowing the client to work on issues that are the focus of therapy between sessions. Homework can also be looked at as a tool for more fully engaging the client in the treatment process. Assignments place more responsibility on the client to resolve his or her presenting problems, belaying the expectation that some clients tend to experience—that the therapist alone can cure him or her. For some, it even may bring a sense of self-empowerment.

Another added benefit of homework is that these assignments give the client the opportunity to implement and evaluate insights or coping behaviors that have been discussed in therapy sessions. Practice, if you will, can make perfect—or at least heighten awareness of various issues. Furthermore, homework can increase the expectation for the client to follow through with making changes rather than just talking about change. Exercises require participation, which can create a sense that the client is taking active steps toward change. Alternatively, homework can also set the stage for trial experiences for the client; those experiences can be brought back to the next session for processing. As a result, modifications can be made to the thoughts, feelings, or behaviors as the homework is processed in the therapy session.

Occasionally treatment processes can become vague and abstract. By adding focus and structure, homework assignments can reenergize treatment. Moreover, homework can increase the clients' motivation to change because it gives them something specific to work on. Two other additional benefits include the increased involvement of family members and significant others in the client's treatment by way of assignments that call for the participation of others, and the promotion of more efficient treatment by encouraging the client to actively develop insights, positive self-talk, and coping behaviors between therapy sessions. Consequently, many clients express increased satisfaction with the treatment process when homework is given. They are pleased to be given something active to do which facilitates the change process, and it reinforces their sense of control over the problem. Because of these advantages, the assignment of therapeutic homework has become increasingly prevalent.

HOW TO USE THIS HOMEWORK PLANNER

Creating homework assignments and developing the printed forms for recording responses can be a time-consuming process. *The Brief Family Therapy Homework Planner,* which follows the lead of psychotherapeutic interventions suggested in *The Family Therapy Treatment Planner* (Dattilio & Jongsma, Wiley, 2000), was written to provide a menu of homework assignments that can easily be photocopied. In addition to the printed format, the assignments in this Planner are provided on a disk to allow the therapist to open them in a word processor and then print them out as is or quickly custom-tailor them to suit each client's individual needs and the therapist's style.

The assignments are grouped under presenting problems that are typical of those found in an adolescent population. These presenting problems are cross-referenced to most of the presenting problems found in *The Family Therapy Treatment Planner.* Although these assignments were originally created with a specific presenting problem in mind, don't feel locked in by specific behavioral problems. Included with each exercise is a cross-referenced list of suggested presenting problems for which the assignment may be appropriate and useful. This cross-referenced list can assist you in applying the assignments to other situations that may be relevant to your client's particular presenting problem. A broader cross-reference of assignments is found in the appendix, "Alternate Assignments for Presenting Problems." Review this list to find relevant assignments beyond those found in the exact presenting problem chapter in which you are interested.

ABOUT THE ASSIGNMENTS

Some of the assignments are designed for the parents of an adolescent who is in treatment; others are only for the client; still others are designed for the parents and adolescent to complete together. Therapists will have to introduce the therapy assignment with varying degrees of detail and client preparation. Recommendations regarding this preparation are made on the title page of each assignment under the heading "Suggestions for Processing This Exercise with Client."

When using this sourcebook, clinical judgment must be used to assess the appropriate developmental level necessary for a specific assignment, as well as whether the homework focuses on relevant issues for the client. The title page of each assignment contains a section on "Goals of the Exercise," which should guide you in your selection of relevant homework for your client. Remember, all assignments can be modified as necessary for the individual client.

CARRYING OUT THE ASSIGNMENT

It is recommended that you first peruse the entire book of homework assignments to familiarize yourself with the broad nature of the types and focuses of the homework. When the time arrives, select a specific assignment under a presenting problem and review the list of homework objectives. Assigning therapy homework is just a beginning step in the therapy treatment process. Carrying out the assignment requires an exploration, on your end as well as the client's, to find the conclusions at which the client has arrived. What are the results? Was this assignment useful to the client? Can it be redesigned or altered for better results? Feel free to examine and search for new and creative ways to actively engage your client in participating in this homework process.

LOUIS J. BEVILACQUA
FRANK M. DATTILIO

ACKNOWLEDGMENTS

The challenging task of assembling a manuscript such as this one is not possible without the contributions of many individuals working on the sidelines.

First and foremost, we would like to thank the many families who have provided us with our vast experiences during our years of clinical work. This has allowed us to generate a number of effective assignments that are contained in the text. It is only after much trial and error that we are able to sort out what works and what does not and convey it in a manner that can be applied clinically.

In addition, we would like to give hearty thanks to our expert typist, Carol Jaskolka, who has devoted a great deal of time and energy to preparing the manuscript and assembling the various chapters. For this, we are greatly indebted to her. Many thanks also go to our publisher Kelly Franklin and executive editor Peggy Alexander, at John Wiley & Sons. We are grateful to them for their trust and patience in us to provide a first-rate manuscript.

Last, our greatest thanks are extended to our own families, who have been undyingly supportive to us as we practice what we preach, despite the time and attention they were deprived of during the completion of this manuscript.

INTRODUCTION

Congratulations on deciding to purchase this book. This is probably one of the best investments that you can make as a family therapist, particularly in light of the ever-increasing need for treatment planning and documentation in your clinical practice.

Although all therapeutic modalities do not utilize homework assignments in the same way, the majority of them do find it necessary to recommend assignments as a means of following through with the facilitation of change. In fact, homework assignments are probably one of the main ingredients to solidifying change in the psychotherapeutic process. This is most likely due to the fact that a significant portion of change actually occurs once the clients leave the therapist's office. The therapist's recommendations or affects in the process of treatment are only as good as the extent to which clients employ them.

Thus, homework assignments help the therapy gel, since the majority of clients' time is spent outside of the therapeutic hour. This is true now more than ever in an age where increasing emphasis has been placed on short-term psychotherapy and the need for structured treatment and independent assignments.

It is with this philosophy that we offer the contents of this homework planner for the contemporary family therapist. Family therapy as much as any other therapeutic intervention views homework as a crucial part of enacting what is learned in treatment (Dattilio, Epstein, and Baucom, 1998). Homework that is specifically germane to the content of the therapy session, in our opinion, is essential in assuring change.

The specific homework assignments in this text have been specially tailored to help the family therapist guide family members in achieving lasting change. They are closely keyed to the topics covered in the adjoining *Family Psychotherapy Treatment Planner* (Dattilio and Jongsma, 2000) and have been designed to be user-friendly with a number of contemporary modalities of family therapy.

We have made a concerted effort to be as comprehensive and eclectic as possible in order to provide you with sundry exercises that you may implement in treatment regardless of your particular approach.

USING THIS BOOK TO ITS FULLEST

First and foremost, these homework assignments are grouped under presenting problems that correspond to material in *The Family Psychotherapy Treatment Planner* (Dattilio and Jongsma, 2000). These are typical of the types of problems that most families encounter and are based on their reasons for seeking treatment.

Each chapter begins with a note to the therapist on how to suggest the use of a particular exercise. It should be noted that this is not intended to be a self-help book, but rather its contents are designed to be used by professionally trained family therapists as therapeutic prescriptions for bolstering techniques and facilitating change with families. It is therefore only to be used under the guidance of a professionally trained therapist.

Each homework assignment is easy to reproduce and may be distributed at the beginning or end of therapy sessions. We encourage each therapist to feel free to embellish or modify the homework assignment in order to fit the particular case that you are working with. We realize that families in many ways are analogous to fingerprints in that although they often look identical, no two are alike. Therefore, alterations and modifications become necessary, and assignments may be most effective if made to fit each family.

We also suggest that these homework assignments be used as stepping stones to generate your own homework assignments by simply inserting the disk into your computer and altering it as you see fit, making substantial or minor changes. These homework assignments can also be reduced to be administered to selected family members or the family in its entirety.

We are also strong supporters of what cognitive-behavior therapists refer to as "collaborative empiricism." Therefore, we strongly believe in working along with family members to develop the homework assignments, collaboratively using their input as a key ingredient in the homework assignment. What is important is that the homework assignment becomes tailored and germane to the specific problems that the family is experiencing. To help you in this matter, there is also a broader cross-reference of assignments, which can be found in the Appendix under "Alternate Assignments for Presenting Problems." These may provide you with some additional suggestions for altering your assignments.

Above all, we defer to the family therapist to use his/her clinical judgment as to knowing when to implement such homework assignments. Obviously, homework is not for everyone, and only the clinical professional can determine the right time and place to make suggestions for homework assignments.

It is very important that you read through the entire contents and familiarize yourself with each assignment before actually suggesting it to a family. This will be particularly important during your initial use of this book, when you may not yet be familiar with the types of reactions and results that will be obtained as a result of the assignments.

IMPLEMENTING THE ASSIGNMENT

We suggest that in implementing these assignments, the therapist keep a number of things in mind. First, it is important to think about how you wish to suggest the use of assignments during the course of therapy and what point in the treatment process may be a good time to intervene. This, of course, varies and will be left up to your clinical judgment. Once you decide to utilize the assignments, then it is suggested that you use your own style in approaching your clients, but in any case be sure to go over each assignment with them so that they understand exactly what the rationale for the assignment is, and more importantly, that they know exactly what they are to do. We often find that clients will sometimes nod their heads as though they understand when, in fact, they are confused about the assignment, but are reluctant to speak up for various reasons. In order for the clients to derive the maximum benefits, it will be important that you make sure that they understand the assignment. It is also important to secure an agreement from everyone to try the assignment. You may very often encounter situations in which several family members think an assignment is a good idea and agree to it, while others do not. Again, we defer to your clinical judgment as to whether to push the issue or not, but it is important to attempt to secure some type of unified agreement to at least try the assignment. The more agreement that you achieve among family members about trying the assignment, the more likely the assignments are to be successful.

Following up on the results is obviously very important, and we strongly recommend that this be considered an agenda for the subsequent visit, unless of course the family requests more time to complete the task. Making sure that you follow up on the results will also provide an indirect message to the family that these assignments are important and are not administered in order to fill time or cosmetically appear as though you just want to give them something to do.

From time to time during the course of homework assignments, therapists will encounter difficulties. One of the most common problems is failure by the family to complete the assignment. This often occurs even despite the fact that the family has agreed to the assignment and acknowledged that it is a good idea.

It is important to understand that often the most common reason for failing to complete homework assignments is resistance. This resistance may have its roots in more complicated dynamics of the family, or it may be as simple as the fact that the assignments are being referred to as "homework." Sometimes people have difficulty with this word because of the negative connotations that the term "homework" carries during the course of early education and upbringing. We therefore suggest that you consider changing the word *homework* to either *task* or *experiment*. We often find that it is very well received when we suggest to a family, "Suppose we try an experiment?" There is something intriguing about this term, and for many its use is less threatening or dictatorial than the word "homework."

It is also important to keep an open mind about how to handle failures to complete the task assignments. It has been said more than once that we can clearly learn from our failures as well as from our successes. Perhaps families who fail to complete the task assignments may be providing us with important information as to "why" (e.g., difficulties with communication, working together as a unit, or resistance to an activity that may yield change). Regardless of the reason, it is important to explore both the dynamics behind failure and the alternatives that may be utilized. Upon discussing this in detail, the therapist may decide to reassign the same or a different exercise, or to forfeit the idea completely until another time.

Last, the type and nature of the task assignment may contribute to some reasons for resistance or failure. If this is the case, once explored with the family, perhaps the use of an alternative assignment may be in order. Again, the reader is referred to the Appendix for alternative assignments for the presenting problems.

It is our hope that this book will prove to be an invaluable resource for you in your challenging work with families. Above all, it is also our goal that the following exercises may help you to expand your repertoire in the same vein that it may help your families grow as well.

LOUIS J. BEVILACQUA
FRANK M. DATTILIO

ADDICTIONS

STAYING CLEAN

GOALS OF THE EXERCISE

1. Identify triggers to relapse.
2. Provide greater understanding and insight for nonaddicted family members.

ADDITIONAL HOMEWORK THAT MAY BE APPLICABLE TO STAYING CLEAN

• Eating Disorders	What Am I Thinking?	Page 124
• Suicide Attempts	Creating a Positive Outlook	Page 204

ADDITIONAL PROBLEMS FOR WHICH THIS EXERCISE MAY BE USEFUL

- Anxiety
- Social Problems*
- Stealing Behaviors*

SUGGESTIONS FOR PROCESSING THIS EXERCISE WITH CLIENT

When a member of the family has an addiction it affects the entire family in a variety of ways. There are many ways in which family members can help the individual who is in recovery. One of the steps to recovery is for the addicted individual to identify specific triggers to substance use. After identifying these triggers, they should be shared with the family. This provides greater insight and understanding for the nonaddicted members of the family. It also helps the recovering individual begin to take control of his/her life by becoming aware of and acknowledging those factors that lead his or her behaviors to be out of control.

In the exercise that follows, the recovering member is asked to answer a number of questions. Once completed, his/her answers should be shared with the therapist during an individual session and then with other family members.

---

* These problems are not specifically discussed in detail in this volume.

STAYING CLEAN

FOR RECOVERING FAMILY MEMBER

One of the best ways for you to prevent relapsing is to become aware of the triggers to your need to use. Once you can identify these triggers, you may begin to feel more control over your life. Knowing what the triggers are can aid you in developing a stronger preventative plan to relapse. In this exercise, answer the following questions. Once completed, this exercise should be shared during an individual session with the therapist and then with other family members.

Describe the last five situations in which you used substance by answering the following questions:

1. Who were you with? _____
   _____
   _____

2. Where were you? _____
   _____
   _____

3. What time of the day was it? _____
   _____
   _____

4. How were you feeling before you chose to get high? _____
   _____
   _____

5. What were you thinking about before you got high? _____
   _____
   _____

6. What were your thoughts/feelings about that person or those people you were with?
   _____
   _____

7. What did the substance do for you? _____

_____

_____

8. What were you able to avoid by using the substance (i.e., feelings, hassles, people, situations, responsibilities)? _____

_____

_____

9. How much do you believe that others are responsible for you getting high? _____

_____

_____

WHAT ELSE CAN I DO?

GOALS OF THE EXERCISE

1. Identify alternative strategies to dealing with triggers to relapse.
2. Create reasons to remain clean.
3. List those thoughts and behaviors that you need to change.

ADDITIONAL HOMEWORK THAT MAY BE APPLICABLE TO CLIENTS WITH AN ADDICTION

*   Eating Disorders   What Am I Thinking?   Page 124
*   Suicide Attempts   Creating a Positive Outlook   Page 204

ADDITIONAL PROBLEMS IN WHICH THIS EXERCISE MAY BE USEFUL

*   Eating Disorders
*   School Problems
*   Stealing Behaviors*

SUGGESTIONS FOR PROCESSING THIS EXERCISE WITH CLIENT

Once triggers are identified, new coping skills and strategies must be implemented to reduce the chances of relapse. Addiction is overwhelmingly powerful and can destroy lives and families. This cannot be emphasized enough. When an individual in recovery begins to have cravings or experience stress/triggers, the thoughts and desires to use quickly reappear. During these times individuals must be reminded of the benefits of staying clean and that other options are available for dealing with whatever problems they are encountering.

---

* This problem is not specifically discussed in detail in this volume.

WHAT ELSE CAN I DO?

FOR THE RECOVERING FAMILY MEMBER AND HIS/HER FAMILY

As a family project, select a stack of index cards. Each family member should write down one or more reasons s/he doesn't want the recovering member to relapse and how s/he feels about the recovering person when that person is clean. The recovering member should do this as well. In the next family session, each person will take turns reading his or her card aloud.

Another way to help someone remain clean is by instituting "Caring Days."* Every so often, a family member does something caring for the recovering person (as well as for any other family member). The member who is in recovery can also participate by doing something caring for him or herself as well as for someone in the family in order to invoke an ongoing exchange.

---

* This was originally an exercise developed by Richard Stuart (1980) for use with couples. It is adapted here and elsewhere (Dattilio & Jongsma, 2000) to be used with families.

OTHER ADDICTIVE BEHAVIORS

GOALS OF THE EXERCISE

1. Addictive or compulsive behavior is reduced or eliminated.
2. Family members feel that their concerns have been validated by the efforts of the addicted member to follow the activity schedule.

ADDITIONAL HOMEWORK THAT MAY BE APPLICABLE TO CLIENTS WITH AN ADDICTION

- Eating Disorders   What Am I Thinking?   Page 124
- Suicide Attempts   Creating a Positive Outlook   Page 204

ADDITIONAL PROBLEMS FOR WHICH THIS EXERCISE MAY BE USEFUL

- Obsessive Type Behaviors*
- School Problems
- Stealing Behaviors*

SUGGESTIONS FOR PROCESSING THIS EXERCISE WITH CLIENT

When a family member's behavior becomes so excessive or obsessive that it interferes with his/her daily or weekly activities or functioning, it can be an addiction. Various inventories (such as the Daily Activity Sheet or Addictive Behaviors Scale) can be used in order to identify a level of severity. Once this is accomplished and the addictive behavior is identified, family members need the opportunity to voice their perspectives on the negative effects that the addictive behavior has had on the family in general. This can be done in a family session. Usually, family members then want the identified behavior to be eliminated or at least reduced. One way to do this is by following a structured format to regulate behaviors.

---

* These problems are not specifically discussed in detail in this volume.

OTHER ADDICTIVE BEHAVIORS

FOR RECOVERING FAMILY MEMBER

One way for you to reduce or hopefully eliminate addictive or unwanted behaviors is to create a daily activity schedule. Having a daily activity schedule or action plan allows you to schedule activities that you know are good for you. The chart below will help you schedule your time on a weekly basis.

FORM FOR DAILY ACTIVITY SCHEDULE						
Sun.	Mon.	Tues.	Wed.	Thurs.	Fri.	Sat.
8:00						
8:30						
9:00						
9:30						
10:00						
10:30						
11:00						
11:30						
12:00						
12:30						
1:00						
1:30						
2:00						
2:30						

	Sun.	Mon.	Tues.	Wed.	Thurs.	Fri.	Sat.
3:00							
3:30							
4:00							
4:30							
5:00							
5:30							
6:00							
6:30							
7:00							
7:30							
8:00							
8:30							
9:00							

Section II

ADOPTION

THIS IS HOW I FEEL

GOALS OF THE EXERCISE

1. The adopted child expresses feelings associated with being adopted.
2. Adopted child believes other family members understand how he or she is feeling.
3. All family members verbalize positive feelings toward one another.
4. Parents achieve positive feelings about their role as adoptive parents.

ADDITIONAL HOMEWORK THAT MAY BE APPLICABLE TO ADOPTION

Child Sexual Abuse	A Picture Is Worth a Thousand Words (just pictures 1–3)	Page 81
Interracial Family Problems	They're Calling Me a Half-Breed	Page 157
Suicide Attempts	Creating a Positive Outlook	Page 204

ADDITIONAL PROBLEMS FOR WHICH THIS EXERCISE MAY BE USEFUL

Blended Families
Foster Care

SUGGESTIONS FOR PROCESSING THIS EXERCISE WITH CLIENT

One of the most significant issues for a person who has been adopted is the need for acceptance and attachment or belonging. This is often the heart of the reason for why an adoptive child/adolescent experiences struggles and needs to seek treatment.

For younger children, the exercise questions might be answered more easily and with greater depth via drawings or other expressive modalities. For adolescents who do not like to write, ask them to record their responses on an audiotape or via another form of expressive art (i.e., computer).

THIS IS HOW I FEEL

FOR ADOPTIVE CHILD/ADOLESCENT

Being adopted can create a number of different thoughts and feelings. The exercise below will help you to identify and express such thoughts and feelings. If you would rather not write down your responses, try drawing them or recording them on an audio tape.

1. Give three or four reasons why children are adopted? _____
    _____
    _____
    _____
    _____

2. Explain the circumstances of how you were adopted? How did it happen? _____
    _____
    _____
    _____
    _____

3. What type(s) of people adopt children? _____
    _____
    _____
    _____
    _____

4. What type of contact should an adopted child have with his/her biological family?
    _____
    _____
    _____
    _____

5.	When you think about your biological family, what thoughts and feelings do you experience? Would you classify these as positive or as negative thoughts/emotions?

_____

_____

_____

_____

6.	When you think about your adoptive family, what thoughts and feelings do you have? Would you classify these as either positive or negative/thoughts emotions?

_____

_____

_____

_____

MY SAFE PLACE

GOALS OF THE EXERCISE

1. To develop a sense of security and comfort no matter where you are or what time it is.
2. To be able to focus and reassure yourself that you are okay.
3. To be able to access that safe place whenever you feel frightened or insecure.

ADDITIONAL HOMEWORK THAT MAY BE APPLICABLE TO ADOPTION

*   Suicide Attempts   Creating a Positive Outlook   Page 204
*   Interracial Family Problems   They're Calling Me a Half-Breed   Page 157
*   Child Sexual Abuse   A Picture Is Worth a Thousand Words   Page 81
                         (just pictures 1–3)

ADDITIONAL PROBLEMS FOR WHICH THIS EXERCISE MAY BE USEFUL

*   Blended Families
*   Child Sexual Abuse
*   Depression
*   Foster Care

SUGGESTIONS FOR PROCESSING THIS EXERCISE WITH CLIENT

When people feel unaccepted or detached it is often helpful to locate a safe place for them (literally or figuratively). A safe place can be anywhere a person feels protected and able to truly relax without worrying. Through the use of imagery and visualization, a person can ideally access their safe place anytime, day or night, no matter where they are or whom they are with. The following exercise provides a pathway to creating a safe place.

Before this task can be assigned, several sessions must be conducted in order to teach deep breathing and basic relaxation skills. After practicing and learning how to use diaphragmatic breathing,* explore with your client what type of place makes him/her feel

---

* With younger children, this can be learned by blowing bubbles. The slower and longer the breath, the bigger the bubble one can make.

good, comfortable, and calm. (Younger children may express places in which there are lots of activities and games. Redirect them to focus on places that are peaceful and quiet. Such places might be their bedroom or a tree house.) Facilitate the use of their imagination as much as possible.

Once a place is identified, have your client go there at least once before their next appointment and spend approximately 10 to 15 minutes there. Have them record as many details as possible about their safe place.

MY SAFE PLACE

FOR ADOPTIVE CHILD/ADOLESCENT

Feeling safe is a great feeling to have. Sometimes we are lucky enough to have a place where we can go and feel totally protected from anything and everything we don't like. It can be a real place like our room, our tree fort, the park, on our bike. Or, it can be a place we can picture in our mind. A place in which we decide what it looks like, what it smells like, how big or small it is, what is in it, who, if anyone else, gets to visit. For the exercise below, try to think about what makes you feel safe. Where would it be? Try to picture it. Use the questions to describe your safe place.

1. My special safe place is _____
   _____
   _____
   _____
   _____

2. Describe your safe place. (What does it look like? What does it smell like? How big is it? What is in it? What color is it?) _____
   _____
   _____
   _____
   _____

3. I feel safe there because_____
   _____
   _____
   _____
   _____

Section III

ANGER PROBLEMS

WHY AM I SO ANGRY?

GOALS OF THE EXERCISE

1. For family members to identify the sources of their anger.
2. For family members to identify the frequency of becoming angry and what they do.

ADDITIONAL HOMEWORK THAT MAY BE APPLICABLE
TO ANGER PROBLEMS

• Adoption	My Safe Place	Page 14
• Depression	What Am I Thinking When I Am Feeling Depressed?	Page 104
• Suicide Attempts	Creating a Positive Outlook	Page 204

ADDITIONAL PROBLEMS FOR WHICH THIS EXERCISE MAY BE USEFUL

- Anxiety
- Depression

SUGGESTIONS FOR PROCESSING THIS EXERCISE WITH CLIENT

Individuals who have difficulty with managing their anger are oftentimes unaware of just how often they become angry or why. The exercise on the following pages is designed to help such individuals increase their anger awareness. The more awareness they develop the more it will allow them to have greater self-control.

WHY AM I SO ANGRY?

FOR CHILD/ADOLESCENT EXPERIENCING ANGER PROBLEMS

1. For one week, use the chart provided to keep track of the times you become angry.

Date	Time	Trigger	My Reaction	Thoughts or Feelings After

2. Using the chart, identify the three top reasons for your becoming angry.

    A. _____

    _____

    _____

    B. _____

    _____

    _____

    C. _____

    _____

    _____

WHAT HAPPENS WHEN I BECOME ANGRY?

GOALS OF THE EXERCISE

1. To identify the physiological, cognitive, and behavioral signs of anger.
2. To begin to develop a sense of how others perceive an individual's anger.

ADDITIONAL HOMEWORK THAT MAY BE APPLICABLE
TO ANGER PROBLEMS

- Adoption   My Safe Place   Page 14
- Depression   What Am I Thinking When I Am Feeling Depressed?   Page 104
- Suicide Attempts   Creating a Positive Outlook   Page 204

ADDITIONAL PROBLEMS FOR WHICH THIS EXERCISE MAY BE USEFUL

- Anxiety

SUGGESTIONS FOR PROCESSING THIS EXERCISE WITH CLIENT

When people become angry it is important for them to become aware of their bodily reactions, thought patterns, and actual behaviors. By increasing his/her awareness of these undesirable factors, a person can begin to take control and reduce them.

WHAT HAPPENS WHEN I BECOME ANGRY?

FOR CHILD/ADOLESCENT EXPERIENCING ANGER PROBLEMS

For you to change what happens when you become angry, you first need to get in tune with your bodily reactions and thoughts, as well as what you actually do when you become angry. Once you get a handle on these three factors, how you want to change can then be planned. The following exercise will help guide you through what happens when you become angry.

1. After becoming angry, answer the following questions with a "YES" or "NO":

    A. When I was angry I noticed that my heart was pounding harder, faster, or louder.

    _____

    B. When I was angry I noticed my muscles felt tense or tight. _____

    C. This was especially true for my (indicate the part of your body) _____

    _____

    D. When I was angry I noticed my skin felt hotter or became red. _____

    E. When I was angry I could feel the adrenaline rushing through my body._____

    F. Describe any other physiological reaction when you were angry._____

    _____

    _____

2. After becoming angry (or while angry) I was thinking: _____

    _____

    _____

3. When I was angry I (describe what you did) _____

    _____

    _____

4. After I was angry I (describe what you did) _____

    _____

    _____

5. On a scale of 1 to 100, I would rate the level of my anger as _____

6. When I became angry my family probably felt _____
   _____

7. When I became angry my family probably thought _____
   _____

   _____

I DON'T HAVE ANY BRUISES BUT I STILL HURT

GOALS OF THE EXERCISE

1. For family members to identify how they react to anger and conflict.
2. To help such family members feel validated and to affirm the thought that such behavior is inappropriate.

ADDITIONAL HOMEWORK THAT MAY BE APPLICABLE
TO ANGER PROBLEMS

- Adoption   My Safe Place   Pages 14
- Depression   What Am I Thinking When I Am Feeling Depressed?   Pages 104
- Suicide Attempts   Creating a Positive Outlook   Pages 204

ADDITIONAL PROBLEMS FOR WHICH THIS EXERCISE MAY BE USEFUL

- Family Conflicts
- Verbal Abuse

SUGGESTIONS FOR PROCESSING THIS EXERCISE WITH CLIENT

Verbal abuse is as violent and as damaging as physical abuse. Many times, individuals attempt to minimize this damage with thoughts such as, "It's not like I am getting beat." The bruises left from verbal abuse are like scars on the soul. These bruises are internal, in that they get intertwined in how we create our sense of self. The following exercise is intended to help individuals verbalize that such experiences are unwanted and to assist them in learning how to assert themselves. It is intended for all family members who are the victims of such experiences.

I DON'T HAVE ANY BRUISES BUT I STILL HURT

Verbal abuse is as violent and damaging as physical abuse. Many times, you may try to minimize this with thoughts such as, "It's not like I am getting beat." However, the bruises left from verbal abuse are like scars on the soul. Sometimes these bruises hurt even more because these bruises are internal, in that they get intertwined in how we create our sense of self. The following exercise is intended to help you express that such experiences are unwanted and to assist you in learning how to assert yourself.

FOR THE PERSON WHO DIRECTLY RECEIVES THE BRUNT OF VERBAL ABUSE

1. When someone yells at me, calls me names, threatens me, or otherwise puts me down, I feel _____

    _____

    _____

    _____

2. The thoughts I have about myself when someone yells at me, calls me names, threatens me, or otherwise puts me down are: _____

    _____

    _____

    _____

    _____

    _____

3. The thoughts I have about that person who is yelling at me, calling me names, threatening me, or otherwise putting me down are: _____

    _____

    _____

    _____

    _____

    _____

4. The person who hurts me this way the most is: _____

5. Other people who have done this include: _____

_____

_____

_____

_____

6. What I want to say to this person (and these others) is: _____

_____

_____

_____

_____

_____

_____

_____

7. Messages that I tell myself to make me feel better are: _____

_____

_____

_____

_____

_____

8. Things that I can do to make me feel better are: _____

_____

_____

_____

_____

_____

FOR FAMILY MEMBERS WHO OBSERVE (SEE OR HEAR) ANOTHER FAMILY MEMBER BEING VERBALLY ABUSED

1. The feelings I have when I observe someone in my family being yelled at, called names, threatened, or made to feel bad or scared are: _____

_____

_____

2. The thoughts I have when such experiences occur are: _____

    _____

    _____

    _____

    _____

3. The feelings I have regarding the person in my family who is doing the yelling, name-calling, threatening, and so forth are: _____

    _____

    _____

    _____

4. The thoughts I have about the person in my family who is doing the yelling, name-calling, threatening, and so forth are: _____

    _____

    _____

    _____

    _____

5. What I think should be done about this problem is: _____

    _____

    _____

    _____

    _____

    _____

6. What I can say to _____ (person being verbally abused) to make him/her feel better is: _____

    _____

    _____

    _____

    _____

    _____

    _____

GO BLOW OUT SOME CANDLES

GOALS OF THE EXERCISE

1. To begin to develop control over your anger.
2. To learn a way to relax more.

ADDITIONAL HOMEWORK THAT MAY BE APPLICABLE TO ANGER PROBLEMS

ADDITIONAL PROBLEMS FOR WHICH THIS EXERCISE MAY BE USEFUL

- Anxiety

SUGGESTIONS FOR PROCESSING THIS EXERCISE WITH CLIENT

Because anger can be physically dangerous and can lead to the erosion of family life, it is important for individuals to learn how to redirect and reduce such feelings. Once individuals have learned some of the triggers to their anger as well as the physiological, cognitive, and behavioral responses to anger, it is important for them to learn how to redirect and prevent themselves from losing control. The following exercise is designed for any family member who wants to learn to take control over his/her anger.

GO BLOW OUT SOME CANDLES

FOR ANY FAMILY MEMBER WHO WANTS TO CONTROL HIS/HER ANGER

Practice the following exercise at least four times in the next week:

When feeling the initial signs of anger, practice taking a deep breath. To do so, breathe in through your nose. When you do, picture a balloon in your belly that you are trying to blow up. As you exhale through your mouth, count to 3. You can also picture blowing out a candle. Try to blow up 8 to 10 balloons, and blow out 8 to 10 candles.

Section IV

ANXIETY

MY/OUR DAUGHTER IS AFRAID TO GO TO SCHOOL

GOALS OF THE EXERCISE

1. Develop a basic understanding as to why the fear exists.
2. Develop alternative self-talk when feeling afraid to attend school.
3. Identify role of each family member in enabling or compounding the fears of the anxious child.

ADDITIONAL HOMEWORK THAT MAY BE APPLICABLE TO ANXIETY PROBLEMS

• Adoption	My Safe Place	Page 14
• Child Sexual Abuse	A Picture Is Worth a Thousand Words (just pictures 1–3)	Page 81
• Suicide Attempts	Creating a Positive Outlook	Page 204

ADDITIONAL PROBLEMS FOR WHICH THIS EXERCISE MAY BE USEFUL

• Low Self-Esteem*

SUGGESTIONS FOR PROCESSING THIS EXERCISE WITH CLIENT

When a child is afraid of attending school it is important to elicit what specific fears he/she has and why they may have developed. This can be accomplished directly in sessions (i.e., by Socratic questioning). Very often parents try to help a fearful child by giving him/her reassuring statements. However, very often this can actually maintain the anxiety. What is needed is for the child to develop self assurance and some coping skills. To accomplish this, have the child list the various statements he/she makes when feeling frightened. Alongside of each fearful statement, have him/her write a reassuring or countering statement. Copy this or just the counterstatements on an index card. Whenever the child is feeling scared, direct him/her to take out the list and read it. These are referred to as *coping cards*. Whenever the child expresses fear to his/her parent(s), the parent(s) respond by saying, "Remember what you wrote on your coping card." Then have them rate the outcome of their response to the card (e.g., it helped some, a lot, did not help, etc.).

---

* This problem is not specifically discussed in detail in this volume.

MY/OUR DAUGHTER IS AFRAID TO GO TO SCHOOL

FOR PARENTS AND FEARFUL CHILD

Being a parent is the most difficult job in the world. When one of our children is hurting, our initial response is to take care of them, to fix the hurt. When that hurt is a fear of attending school, our natural response is to reassure our child that "everything will be fine" and "you are okay." This usually helps to some degree, but the anxiety returns once you stop the reassurance. To overcome this, your child/adolescent must learn to make self-reassuring statements. This allows them to take control. To accomplish this, have your child/adolescent list the various statements she/he makes when feeling frightened. Alongside of each fearful statement, have them write a reassuring or countering statement. Copy this or just the counterstatements on an index card. Whenever your child/adolescent is feeling scared, direct him/her to take out the list and read it to himself/herself. These are referred to as "coping cards." Whenever your child/adolescent expresses fear to you, respond by saying, "Remember what you wrote on your coping card."

Fearful Self-Talk	Strong Self-Talk	Rate the Outcome
_____	_____	_____
_____	_____	_____
_____	_____	_____
_____	_____	_____
_____	_____	_____
_____	_____	_____

WHEN I FEEL ANXIOUS IT IS LIKE . . .

GOALS OF THE EXERCISE

1. Help the anxious member identify times and situations when/where she/he feels anxious. Use physical examples as much as possible (i.e., butterflies in my stomach).
2. Have family understand the impact that anxiety has on the anxiety-ridden individual.
3. Anxious family member identifies automatic thoughts that accompany anxious feelings as well as the behavior that she/he engages in.
4. Anxious family member learns to practice cognitive restructuring techniques as well as behavioral rehearsal.
5. Family members learn to coach anxious family member in cognitive restructuring techniques and the use of new behaviors.

ADDITIONAL HOMEWORK THAT MAY BE APPLICABLE TO ANXIETY PROBLEMS

• Adoption	My Safe Place	Page 14
• Child Sexual Abuse	A Picture Is Worth a Thousand Words (just pictures 1–3)	Page 81
• Suicide Attempts	Creating a Positive Outlook	Page 204

ADDITIONAL PROBLEMS FOR WHICH THIS EXERCISE MAY BE USEFUL

- Anger
- Depression

SUGGESTIONS FOR PROCESSING THIS EXERCISE WITH CLIENT

When a person feels anxious, one of their main concerns is a fear of losing control. By helping them identify when and in what situations they feel anxious, as well as what they think about and what they do when anxious, you can help them regain a sense of control. It is also important for you to help the other family members who are struggling with feelings of frustration and helplessness over dealing with the anxious family member. By teaching the other family members ways to be helpful and effectively supportive will help in changing how the family as a unit interacts with the anxious member.

WHEN I FEEL ANXIOUS IT IS LIKE . . .

If you are feeling anxious, you most likely want to learn ways to regain control and overcome that fear of losing control. By figuring out the cues or situations in which you tend to feel anxious, as well as what goes through your mind and what you do in those circumstances will give you and your therapist a better understanding of what you need to do differently.

FOR THE ANXIOUS FAMILY MEMBER

Over the next week identify the times/situations, your thoughts/images, and behaviors when feeling anxious.

1. I felt anxious when _____

    _____

    _____

    Describe what went through your mind (i.e., thoughts, images) when you were feeling anxious _____

    _____

    _____

    Describe what you did when you were feeling anxious _____

    _____

    _____

2. I felt anxious when _____

    _____

    _____

    Describe what went through your mind (i.e., thoughts, images) when you were feeling anxious _____

    _____

    _____

    Describe what you did when you were feeling anxious _____

    _____

    _____

3. I felt anxious when _____

_____

_____

Describe what went through your mind (i.e., thoughts, images) when you were feeling anxious _____

_____

_____

Describe what you did when you were feeling anxious _____

_____

_____

4. I felt anxious when _____

_____

_____

Describe what went through your mind (i.e., thoughts, images) when you were feeling anxious _____

_____

_____

Describe what you did when you were feeling anxious _____

_____

_____

Share this with the other family members.

MY MOTHER'S ANXIETY MAKES ME FEEL . . .

GOALS OF THE EXERCISE

1. Have family members identify what it is like for them when their parent(s) is/are anxious.
2. Have family members express their feelings regarding living with an anxiety-ridden person.

ADDITIONAL HOMEWORK THAT MAY BE APPLICABLE TO ANXIETY PROBLEMS

• Adoption	My Safe Place	Page 14
• Child Sexual Abuse	A Picture Is Worth a Thousand Words (just pictures 1–3)	Page 81
• Suicide Attempts	Creating a Positive Outlook	Page 204

ADDITIONAL PROBLEMS FOR WHICH THIS EXERCISE MAY BE USEFUL

- Anger Problems
- Depression

SUGGESTIONS FOR PROCESSING THIS EXERCISE WITH CLIENT

Very often family members are not given a forum to discuss their own thoughts and feelings regarding what it is like for them to live with someone who is frequently anxious. The following exercise is intended to create such a forum.

MY MOTHER'S ANXIETY MAKES ME FEEL . . .

FOR FAMILY MEMBERS

Identify two or three situations in which you observed your parent or spouse being anxious, and then describe how you knew that he/she was anxious.

1. I remember when _____ was _____

    _____

    I could tell _____ was anxious because _____

    _____

    I began thinking and feeling _____

    _____

2. I remember when _____ was _____

    _____

    I could tell _____ was anxious because _____

    _____

    I began thinking and feeling _____

    _____

3. I remember when _____ was _____

    _____

    I could tell _____ was anxious because _____

    _____

    I began thinking and feeling _____

    _____

4. I remember when _____ was _____

    _____

    I could tell _____ was anxious because _____

    _____

    I began thinking and feeling _____

    _____

5. I remember when _____ was _____

    _____

    I could tell _____ was anxious because _____

    _____

    I began thinking and feeling _____

    _____

6. I remember when _____ was _____

    _____

    I could tell _____ was anxious because _____

    _____

    I began thinking and feeling _____

    _____

BEHAVIORAL PROBLEMS IN CHILDREN AND ADOLESCENTS

MY CHILD JUST WON'T LISTEN

GOALS OF THE EXERCISE

1. For parents and children to develop more cooperation with each other.
2. Decrease the amount of conflict and tension within the home/family.
3. Identify the expectations that parents have of their children and that children have of their parents.

ADDITIONAL HOMEWORK THAT MAY BE APPLICABLE TO BEHAVIORAL PROBLEMS IN CHILDREN AND ADOLESCENTS

• Adoption	My Safe Place	Page 14
• Child Sexual Abuse	A Picture Is Worth a Thousand Words (just pictures 1–3)	Page 81
• Depression	What Do Others Value about Me?	Page 106
• School Problems	My Teenager Is Truant	Page 191
• Suicide Attempts	Creating a Positive Outlook	Page 204

ADDITIONAL PROBLEMS FOR WHICH THIS EXERCISE MAY BE USEFUL

- Anger
- Depression
- Substance Abuse

SUGGESTIONS FOR PROCESSING THIS EXERCISE WITH CLIENT

Oftentimes, a child who frequently disobeys and doesn't listen creates and induces anger/ frustration and resentment in his/her parent. Such situations frequently lead to or end in arguments and yelling matches. The following exercise is designed to assist families in developing a sense of control by identifying their view of the conflicts, their thoughts and feelings about the conflicts, and how they would like things to be.

MY CHILD JUST WON'T LISTEN

FOR CHILD AND PARENTS

The following exercise is designed for each of you to regain a sense of control and stabilization within the family. Find a quiet time to think about each of the questions below. Try to be as objective and specific as you can.

1. What do you hate most about the conflicts with your child/parent? _____
   _____
   _____
   _____
   _____
   _____

2. When do these conflicts tend to happen? _____
   _____
   _____
   _____
   _____
   _____

3. What do you try to do to limit or decrease the conflicts? _____
   _____
   _____
   _____
   _____
   _____

4. What does your parent/child do to limit or decrease the conflicts? _____
   _____
   _____
   _____
   _____
   _____

5. What else could your parent/child do to limit or decrease the conflicts? _____

    _____

    _____

    _____

    _____

6. Describe a time in which you were getting along with your child/parent. What were you doing and what were they doing? _____

    _____

    _____

    _____

    _____

7. How did this make you feel? _____

    _____

    _____

8. How hard would it be for you to act the way you described yourself in #6 on a regular basis? _____

    _____ That would be easy

    _____ That would be a little hard

    _____ That would be pretty hard

    _____ That would be next to impossible

9. How would life be if you could act that way more days than not? _____

    _____

    _____

ACTING AS IF

GOALS OF THE EXERCISE

1. To identify the rules or guidelines for living together as a family.
2. To identify the expectations parents have of their child/adolescent and that the child/adolescent has of his/her parents.
3. To decrease the amount of conflict in the home/family.

ADDITIONAL HOMEWORK THAT MAY BE APPLICABLE TO BEHAVIORAL PROBLEMS IN CHILDREN AND ADOLESCENTS

- Adoption | My Safe Place | Page 14
- Child Sexual Abuse | A Picture Is Worth a Thousand Words (just pictures 1–3) | Page 81
- Depression | What Do Others Value about Me? | Page 106
- School Problems | My Teenager Is Truant | Page 191
- Suicide Attempts | Creating a Positive Outlook | Page 204

ADDITIONAL PROBLEMS FOR WHICH THIS EXERCISE MAY BE USEFUL

- Depression
- Family Conflicts

SUGGESTIONS FOR PROCESSING THIS EXERCISE WITH CLIENT

Family members in general are able to easily describe the problems between them. It is important to identify such concerns—but it is equally important to describe how they would want to interact and get along. Once they do so, the therapist should encourage them to put their description into action even if they are just acting.

ACTING AS IF

FOR FAMILY MEMBERS EXPERIENCING CONFLICT

In most families, it is much easier to describe and focus on the problems. Too often families get caught up with how bad things are and get stuck in a pattern or cycle of behaving that way. The following exercise is designed to help you identify problem behaviors that your family is experiencing, and more important, to help you to get a clearer picture of how each of you would like to act as a family. By identifying how each of you would like to be as a family, you take charge of directing and creating a new pattern or cycle of acting as a family.

1. List the problem behaviors, and be as specific as you can. _____
    _____
    _____
    _____
    _____
    _____
    _____
    _____
    _____

2. When do these behaviors typically occur? Try to describe the situation. _____
    _____
    _____
    _____
    _____

3. Describe what your parents/child or adolescent does that tends to make the situation worse. _____
    _____
    _____
    _____
    _____

4. Describe what you do that tends to make the situation worse. _____
    _____
    _____
    _____

5. Describe an ideal time. How would everyone act if you were all getting along?
    _____
    _____
    _____
    _____

6. As a family, pick one day this week in which all of you will plan to act as described in #5 above. Write in the agreed-upon date _____ .

7. Describe your thoughts and feelings when everyone acted this way. _____
    _____
    _____
    _____

WE HAVE TO HAVE SOME KIND OF AGREEMENT

GOALS OF THE EXERCISE

1. To identify the problematic behaviors.
2. To identify the rewards and consequences of behaviors.
3. To help families focus on specific areas of change.
4. To help parents work together and consistently.
5. For children or adolescents to know what is expected.

ADDITIONAL HOMEWORK THAT MAY BE APPLICABLE TO BEHAVIORAL PROBLEMS IN CHILDREN AND ADOLESCENTS

ADDITIONAL PROBLEMS FOR WHICH THIS EXERCISE MAY BE USEFUL

*   Communication Problems
*   Family Conflicts

SUGGESTIONS FOR PROCESSING THIS EXERCISE WITH CLIENT

Sometimes families become overwhelmed with the amount of conflict and tension in the home. It is important to help them zero in on two or three specific areas of change. This allows them to see progress more clearly and is more realistic than trying to change the world all at once.

WE HAVE TO HAVE SOME KIND OF AGREEMENT

FOR PARENTS OF CHILD/ADOLESCENT EXPERIENCING PROBLEMATIC BEHAVIORS

The following exercise is designed to help you reduce the feelings of frustration and being overwhelmed with the "problems" in the family. Identifying two or three specific areas that you want to change allows you to become more focused and keep things more manageable. This will also help you to see progress more clearly.

1. List the problem behaviors and be as specific as you can. Number each one. _____

    _____

    _____

    _____

    _____

    _____

    _____

    _____

    _____

    _____

2. For each numbered behavior above, describe what you expect instead of what you are getting (i.e., polite language in a normal tone of voice, versus cursing whenever he/she is in the house). _____

    _____

    _____

    _____

    _____

    _____

    _____

    _____

    _____

3. List what your child/adolescent views as a reward (i.e., talking on the phone, going outside, using the car, having friends over). _____

    _____

    _____

    _____

    _____

    _____

    _____

4. List what your child/adolescent views as a consequence. _____

    _____

    _____

    _____

    _____

    _____

    _____

5. Pick two or three of the expected behaviors that you want to see more of. _____

    _____

    _____

    _____

    _____

6. Inform your child/adolescent that each day you will be looking to see that she/he is demonstrating such behavior. Each day that you find evidence of this, record and date what you see. Review it with your spouse/partner and then review it with your son/daughter. Explain that evidence equals rewards.

7. Parents are to speak calmly but in a matter-of-fact tone of voice to their child/adolescent when reviewing the evidence.

CHARTING OUR COURSE

GOALS OF THE EXERCISE

1. For younger children to visualize their progress.
2. For parents to visualize their child's progress and help him/her stay focused and consistent.

ADDITIONAL HOMEWORK THAT MAY BE APPLICABLE TO BEHAVIORAL PROBLEMS IN CHILDREN AND ADOLESCENTS

- School Problems   My Teenager Is Truant   Page 191
- Adoption   My Safe Place   Page 14
- Depression   What Do Others Value about Me?   Page 106
- Suicide Attempts   Creating a Positive Outlook   Page 204
- Child Sexual Abuse   A Picture Is Worth a Thousand Words (just   Page 81
                        pictures 1–3)

ADDITIONAL PROBLEMS FOR WHICH THIS EXERCISE MAY BE USEFUL

- Pervasive Developmental Disorder

SUGGESTIONS FOR PROCESSING THIS EXERCISE WITH CLIENT

For younger children, charting expected behavior is very helpful. Using a chart or graph of some type allows them to visualize how well they are doing. Such visual aids are also helpful for parents to notice the positives in their child. This can be a challenge when familys are overly focused on the "problems." The exercise that follows is designed to shift some of the focus onto the positive and to shape more of the expected/desired behavior in children.

CHARTING OUR COURSE

FOR PARENTS AND CHILD

This exercise is designed especially for younger children. Oftentimes a child prefers to "see" that she/he is doing well. Having a visual aid such as a chart also helps you as the parent to "see" more of the positives that your son or daughter is doing.

1. Identify three behaviors that you want your child to do more of (i.e., instead of not talking back, we want Johnny to listen by the second or third prompt). _____
    _____
    _____
    _____

2. Identify two behaviors that are not a problem. These can be behaviors that your child does without much (if any) prodding (i.e., gets dressed by himself/herself). _____
    _____
    _____
    _____

3. With your child, identify three or four rewarding behaviors (i.e., watching TV for 30 minutes; riding a bike; special time with mom and/or dad, such as playing a board game or reading a book together). _____
    _____
    _____
    _____

4. Put the list of rewards on a separate sheet of paper.
5. Use the following chart to fill in the information in the column for behavior as identified in items 1 and 2 above.

Behavior	Sun.	Mon.	Tues.	Wed.	Thurs.	Fri.	Sat.
Totals							

6. Each day, or evening, sit with your child and review the day. For each desired behavior displayed, a sticker, check-mark, or smiley face should be entered into the corresponding block on the chart.

7. The bottom row is used for adding up the number of stickers, check-marks, or smiley faces.

8. The total number of desired behaviors for each day or for each week can be traded in for rewards identified in item 4.

Section VI

BIPOLAR DISORDER

MY MOM JUST WON'T STAY ON HER MEDICATION

GOALS FOR THIS EXERCISE

1. Increase the consistency of medication adherence.
2. Family members develop an understanding of how they can be a support.

ADDITIONAL HOMEWORK THAT MAY BE APPLICABLE TO BIPOLAR DISORDER

• Adoption	My Safe Place	Page 14
• Depression	What Am I Thinking When I Am Feeling Depressed?	Page 104

ADDITIONAL PROBLEMS FOR WHICH THIS EXERCISE MAY BE USEFUL

- Anxiety
- Depression

SUGGESTIONS FOR PROCESSING THIS EXERCISE WITH CLIENT

The most frequent treatment for a person with bipolar disorder is medication. This, however, is frequently the most difficult part of the treatment. Individuals with bipolar disorder oftentimes do not want to stop feeling the energy and excitement they experience during a manic phase. As a result, helping them to consistently take their medication can be a challenge.

MY MOM JUST WON'T STAY ON HER MEDICATION

Having to continuously take medication can become very frustrating. Many times, you probably wish you could just stop—and perhaps you do stop. The following exercise is designed to help you and your family to identify and get out some of their thoughts and feelings regarding taking medication and not taking it.

FOR THE FAMILY MEMBER WHO NEEDS TO BE TAKING MEDICATION

1. Describe your thoughts and feelings about having to take medication. _____
    _____
    _____
    _____
    _____

2. Describe your thoughts and feelings when you want to stop taking your medication. What is going on in your life during such times?_____
    _____
    _____
    _____
    _____

3. Give some reasons why it is okay to stop taking your medication. _____
    _____
    _____
    _____
    _____

4. Give some reasons why it is **not** okay to stop taking your medication. _____
    _____
    _____
    _____
    _____

5. Describe how you feel after not taking your medication for a few days, a week, or a month. _____
_____
_____

6. How is your relationship with family members affected when you do not take your medication on a consistent basis?_____
_____
_____
_____

7. Describe how this makes you feel. _____
_____
_____

8. Describe how your family responds to you when you take your medication on a consistent basis. _____
_____
_____

9. Describe how this makes you feel. _____
_____
_____

FOR FAMILY MEMBERS

1. Describe how your _____ acts when she/he is taking her/his medication regularly. _____
_____
_____

2. How does this make you feel? _____
_____
_____

3. Describe how you tend to act toward _____ during such times.
_____
_____
_____
_____

4. Describe how your _____ acts when she/he is **not** taking her/his medication regularly. _____
_____
_____

5. How does this make you feel? _____
    _____
    _____

6. Describe how you react to your _____ when he/she is not taking his/her
    medication. _____
    _____
    _____

7. Does this help the situation or make it worse? Describe. _____
    _____
    _____

8. Ask your _____ how you could be a support to him/her. Record the
    response here. _____
    _____
    _____

BLAMING

DON'T LOOK AT ME, ASK HIM

GOALS OF THE EXERCISE

1. For family members to take responsibility for their words and actions.
2. To reduce the frequency and intensity of blaming situations.
3. To encourage positive interactions.

ADDITIONAL HOMEWORK THAT MAY BE APPLICABLE TO BLAMING

*   Depression   What Am I Thinking When I Am Feeling Depressed?   Page 104
*   Suicide Attempts   Creating a Positive Outlook   Page 204

ADDITIONAL PROBLEMS FOR WHICH THIS EXERCISE MAY BE USEFUL

*   Anger

SUGGESTIONS FOR PROCESSING THIS EXERCISE WITH CLIENT

The following exercise is designed to help individuals take note of their own behaviors (i.e., when they engage in blaming others). By increasing self-monitoring, individuals are more likely to reduce negative behaviors. Individuals are also more likely to begin to develop a sense of empathy for those they hurt.

DON'T LOOK AT ME, ASK HIM

FOR ALL FAMILY MEMBERS

Each family member is to write two letters (i.e., Dear Jane,). In the first letter, describe your thoughts and feelings regarding why you were blaming or pointing a finger at someone else. In the second letter, describe some of the thoughts and feelings of the person you are blaming.

1. The first letter is to justify why the individual who is blaming is upset and pointing a finger at someone else. This letter must use "I" statements such as "I feel angry when I can't find my things." In describing what happened, "I" statements must also be used. For example, "I looked all around the house and could not find my _____. That's when I saw _____ sitting in the chair with what I feel was a smirk on his face. It made me think that he was laughing at me."

2. The second letter is to write why the other person (who was being blamed) should feel upset. This letter must be like an attorney arguing his/her client's case. This letter is to focus solely on how the person who was being blamed feels, thinks, and perceives the situation. For example, "He was watching me run around the house, screaming, yelling, and looking for a pen. It was not his pen and he did tell me to use another pen. He was busy trying to complete his own work. He felt angry that I was accusing him of something even though there was no proof."

THE BLAMING JAR

GOALS OF THE EXERCISE

1. To increase the level of self-monitoring for the individuals who are engaging in blaming others.
2. To decrease the amount of blaming others.

ADDITIONAL HOMEWORK THAT MAY BE APPLICABLE TO BLAMING PROBLEMS

*   Depression   What Am I Thinking When I Am Feeling Depressed?   Page 104
*   Suicide Attempts   Creating a Positive Outlook   Page 204

ADDITIONAL PROBLEMS FOR WHICH THIS EXERCISE MAY BE USEFUL

*   Behavioral Problems (i.e., "Cursing Jar")

SUGGESTIONS FOR PROCESSING THIS EXERCISE WITH CLIENT

The "Blaming Jar" can be used to decrease almost any undesired behavior (e.g., cursing, being late). The purpose is to hold the person accountable for the undesired behavior. Using the Blaming Jar within a family setting increases the likelihood of a person being held accountable because of the additional people watching.

THE BLAMING JAR

FOR ALL FAMILY MEMBERS

This exercise can be in place for several weeks. In fact, it is better to have all family members agree to a three- or four-week contract. During this time, any individual who blames someone else without proof of his/her statements must pay a quarter or dollar to the jar. At the end of the three or four weeks, the money is used to treat the family (e.g., renting a video which all can watch, buying everyone ice cream).

For younger children or those who are not earning any money, instead of putting in a quarter/dollar, they are to write their name and that of the person they were blaming on a piece of paper and put that into the jar. Each week, these individuals are to do something for the person they blamed (e.g., help with an older brother or sisters' chore).

WHAT'S MY JOB?

GOALS OF THE EXERCISE

1. To evenly divide the household responsibilities among all family members.
2. To clearly define each person's responsibility.

ADDITIONAL HOMEWORK THAT MAY BE APPLICABLE TO BLAMING PROBLEMS

- Depression   What Am I Thinking When I Am Feeling Depressed?   Page 104
- Suicide Attempts Creating a Positive Outlook   Page 204

ADDITIONAL PROBLEMS FOR WHICH THIS EXERCISE MAY BE USEFUL

- Behavioral Problems
- Communication Problems

SUGGESTIONS FOR PROCESSING THIS EXERCISE WITH CLIENT

Many times family members complain about other members not helping out around the house. The following exercise is designed to help families break things down into specific duties or responsibilities for each person.

WHAT'S MY JOB?

FOR ALL FAMILY MEMBERS

Family members are to identify the basic household responsibilities and the persons who are to perform them (e.g., who takes out the trash and when, who feeds the cat and when, who puts the kids to bed and when, who does what yard work and when). This information can be put into a chart like the example provided here or simply listed on the calendar. It should then be displayed where all family members can easily view it. The best place is usually in the kitchen.

Household Responsibilities **Family Member**

1. _____ _____

2. _____ _____

3. _____ _____

4. _____ _____

5. _____ _____

6. _____ _____

7. _____ _____

8. _____ _____

9. _____ _____

10. _____ _____

Family Chore Chart

Sun.		Mon.		Tues.		Wed.		Thurs.	
Name	Chore	Name	Chore	Name	Chore	Name	Chore	Name	Chore

Section VIII

BLENDED FAMILIES

I HAVE TOO MANY PARENTS

GOALS OF THE EXERCISE

1. Family members accept responsibility for the adjustment that comes with joining a new family.
2. Family members agree to make exceptions in order to live together harmoniously.
3. Family members explore some of the myths about blended families.

ADDITIONAL HOMEWORK THAT MAY BE APPLICABLE TO BLENDED FAMILIES

ADDITIONAL PROBLEMS FOR WHICH THIS EXERCISE MAY BE USEFUL

- Adoption

SUGGESTIONS FOR PROCESSING THIS EXERCISE WITH CLIENT

Among the most common reactions to blended families are feelings of resentment and the issue of acceptance. It is important for family members to feel that they can express such feelings and thoughts freely. But these are usually difficult for parents to hear and sometimes difficult for children/adolescents to articulate. The following exercise is designed for an existing blended family that needs to commence with this process. This can also be used for a family that is in transition and is about to become a blended family.

I HAVE TOO MANY PARENTS

FOR FAMILY MEMBERS IN A NEW BLENDED FAMILY

Whether one of your parents has already remarried or is about to remarry, it is important for you to be able to express your thoughts and feelings regarding this matter. The following exercise will help you in expressing such thoughts and feelings. Answer the questions that follow as best you can.

1. What are your thoughts and feelings about each family member (natural/step/foster/adoptive)? _____

    _____

    _____

    _____

    _____

2. Identify one to two situations or events (for each member) that influenced you to feel the way that you do. _____

    _____

    _____

    _____

    _____

    _____

    _____

    _____

    _____

    _____

3. What do you believe their feelings are about you? _____

    _____

    _____

    _____

    _____

    _____

4. Identify one or two situations or times that made you think in such a way. (Do this for each family member.) _____

    _____

    _____

    _____

    _____

    _____

    _____

    _____

    _____

5. How did you learn that you were going to have another family? _____

    _____

    _____

    _____

    _____

    _____

    _____

6. What was your worst fear about becoming part of a blended family? _____

    _____

    _____

    _____

    _____

    _____

    _____

7. What is it about this entire thing that makes you uneasy? Angry? Sad? Happy? Scared? _____

    _____

    _____

    _____

    _____

    _____

    _____

8. What does it mean to you to have "stepfamily" members? _____
_____
_____
_____
_____
_____
_____

9. What does this mean about your biological or "natural" family?_____
_____
_____
_____
_____
_____
_____

10. What do you do to make it difficult to get along as a stepfamily unit?_____
_____
_____
_____
_____
_____
_____

11. Name at least two behaviors that you can do to make things better. List some pros
    and cons to doing this. _____
_____
_____
_____
_____
_____

12. Share your responses to this exercise in your next family session.

WE NEED TO AGREE

GOALS OF THE EXERCISE

1. All parents (step, biological, foster, and adoptive) agree to cooperate and work together in the best interest of the children.
2. Children feel greater security and a sense of stability.

ADDITIONAL HOMEWORK THAT MAY BE APPLICABLE TO BLENDED FAMILIES

• Adoption	My Safe Place	Page 14
• Suicide Attempts	Creating a Positive Outlook	Page 204
• Child Sexual Abuse	A Picture Is Worth a Thousand Words (just pictures 1–3)	Page 81

ADDITIONAL PROBLEMS FOR WHICH THIS EXERCISE MAY BE USEFUL

• Adoption

SUGGESTIONS FOR PROCESSING THIS EXERCISE WITH CLIENT

Another common difficulty is for divorced parents to continue acting as a unified team. It is sometimes beneficial to have a session with the parents (including stepparents) to identify and discuss parenting differences. Although this is no easy task, it is suggested that you create a contract that all sign in order to reinforce the commitment of getting along. You may want to include the following areas:

1. Visitation schedule
2. Standard house rules
3. Expectations regarding schoolwork
4. Expectations regarding behaviors

WE NEED TO AGREE

FOR PARENTS IN A DIVORCED OR REMARRIED FAMILY

Being in a divorced or remarried family can be difficult for lots of reasons. You can reduce the difficulties by working together. As parents, it is especially important for you to both be on the same page with each other. Regardless of whether you are married to each other or not, you are both still parents to your children. One of the ways you can make things easier on yourself as well as on the rest of the family is to work together. You are probably saying, "If we could do that we wouldn't have gotten divorced!" You are right. But sometimes it can actually be easier to work together when you are no longer married to or living with each other. The following exercise is designed to help you start the process of working together to reduce your own level of stress (as well as everyone else's).

1. Complete the following schedule for visitation.

	Sunday	Monday	Tuesday	Wednesday	Thursday	Friday	Saturday
Pick-Up Time							
Drop-Off Time							

Once you have agreed on this schedule, give a copy to each child and keep one for yourself.

2. Identify house rules (i.e., dinner is at 6:00 P.M.; curfew is at 9:00 P.M.; and homework is to be done before you go outside or have friends over). The more that your house rules match up with your ex-spouses, the more consistency (and less confusion) there is for your children. A copy of the house rules should then be given to each child (and keep one for yourself).

Dad's House Rules

1. _____
2. _____
3. _____
4. _____
5. _____
6. _____
7. _____

Mom's House Rules

1. _____
2. _____
3. _____
4. _____
5. _____
6. _____
7. _____

Ideally, these two lists can be traded in for one list labeled "Parents' House Rules."

3. Describe your expectations for school (i.e., You need to maintain at least a "C" average in all of your subjects; Homework is to be done before any social activities). Your children should also be able to voice their input to this. Each child should have his or her own list of expectations.

Dad's Expectations for School

1. _____
2. _____
3. _____
4. _____
5. _____

Mom's Expectations for School

1. _____
2. _____
3. _____
4. _____
5. _____

Ideally, these two lists can be traded in for one list labeled "Parents' Expectations for School."

4. Describe the type of behavior you expect of each other (this includes parents with kids as well as kids with parents). For example, "When we speak to each other, we are to speak calmly and with an inside voice and without any cursing or name-calling."

Dad's Expectations of How We Should Treat Each Other

1. _____
2. _____
3. _____
4. _____
5. _____
6. _____
7. _____

Mom's Expectations of How We Should Treat Each Other

1. _____
2. _____
3. _____
4. _____
5. _____
6. _____
7. _____

Ideally, these two lists can be traded in for one list labeled "Parents' Expectations of How We Should Treat Each Other."

CHILD SEXUAL ABUSE

GETTING IT OUT

GOALS OF THE EXERCISE

1. To begin a process of healing.
2. To identify and express thoughts and feelings regarding the abuse.

ADDITIONAL HOMEWORK THAT MAY BE APPLICABLE TO CHILD SEXUAL ABUSE

ADDITIONAL PROBLEMS IN WHICH THIS EXERCISE MAY BE USEFUL

- Domestic Violence*
- Marital Affair*
- Physical Abuse

SUGGESTIONS FOR PROCESSING THIS EXERCISE WITH CLIENT

When a child has been sexually abused, other family members need to express their own thoughts and feelings about what happened. This helps them to be available emotionally to comfort the child who has been abused. When the perpetrator is a family member who lives in the house, oftentimes the home environment is similar to having an elephant in the living room: Everyone walks around it. You need to get the family to express their thoughts, feelings, and expectations that they have of each other and especially the perpetrator. Each family member has his/her own story, which needs to be expressed and heard. The following questions can help in accomplishing this.

---

* These problems are not specifically discussed in detail in this volume.

GETTING IT OUT

It is a tragedy whenever a child is sexually abused. It takes a lot of time and support to overcome such an experience. As a family, in order to provide that support, each of you must be able to get a handle on your thoughts and feelings. This is also true for the person who was abused. For you to move from victim to survivor, you need to process this experience. The following exercise is a place to start for each of you to identify and express your thoughts and feelings.

FOR THE NONABUSED FAMILY MEMBERS

1. How did I feel about _____ (person abused) before I knew s/he was abused? _____

_____

_____

_____

2. How did I feel about _____ (perpetrator) before I knew he/she committed the abuse? _____

_____

_____

_____

3. How do I feel now about _____ (person who was abused)? _____

_____

_____

_____

4. How do I feel now about _____ (perpetrator)? _____

_____

_____

_____

5. What do I think about what happened? _____

_____

_____

_____

6. What questions does it raise in my mind?_____
_____
_____
_____

7. How has the abuse changed my relationship with _____ (person abused)?
_____
_____
_____
_____

8. How has my relationship changed with _____ (perpetrator)? _____
_____
_____
_____
_____

9. What is the worst thing that the abuse has done to the family? _____
_____
_____
_____
_____

10. How do I see my family overcoming this experience?_____
_____

FOR THE PERSON WHO WAS ABUSED

1. How did I feel about the person who abused me before the abuse?_____
_____
_____
_____
_____
_____

2. How do I feel about that person now?_____
_____
_____
_____
_____
_____

3. How did I feel about myself before the abuse? _____
_____
_____
_____
_____
_____

4. How do I feel about myself now? _____
_____
_____
_____
_____
_____

5. What do I think about what happened? What questions does it raise in my mind?
_____
_____
_____
_____
_____

6. How has the abuse changed my relationship with the perpetrator? How do I feel about this? _____
_____
_____
_____
_____
_____

7. How has the abuse changed my relationship with the other family members? How do I feel about this? _____
_____
_____
_____
_____
_____

8. What was the worst thing about the abuse? _____
_____
_____
_____
_____
_____

9. If there was physical contact, how do you feel about your body? _____
_____
_____
_____
_____
_____

10. How do I see myself overcoming what happened to me? _____
_____
_____
_____
_____
_____

11. What is the best thing about me? _____
_____
_____
_____
_____
_____

I GOTTA STOP THINKING THIS WAY

GOALS OF THE EXERCISE

1. Identify the common thinking errors and develop more adaptive self-talk.
2. To begin a process of healing.

ADDITIONAL HOMEWORK THAT MAY BE APPLICABLE TO CHILD SEXUAL ABUSE

ADDITIONAL PROBLEMS FOR WHICH THIS EXERCISE MAY BE USEFUL

- Domestic Violence*
- Physical Abuse*

SUGGESTIONS FOR PROCESSING THIS EXERCISE WITH CLIENT

When a child has been abused, a range of emotions of varying levels of intensity quickly develop. These start when the abuse starts. The following exercise lists some of the more common thoughts that arise. Have your client identify any that apply to him/her and generate alternative, more adaptive thoughts.

---

* These problems are not specifically discussed in detail in this volume.

I GOTTA STOP THINKING THIS WAY

FOR THE PERSON WHO WAS ABUSED

This exercise is designed to help you rid yourself of negative thoughts about what happened to you. The list of faulty beliefs/thoughts is based on the thoughts/beliefs held and reported frequently by others who have also been abused like you. See if you can offer alternative and more positive thoughts/beliefs for each one listed here.

Faulty Beliefs/Thoughts   **More Realistic/Positive Thoughts**

1. It was my fault.   _____

2. I can't trust others.   _____

3. I can't trust myself.   _____

4. I am bad.   _____

5. My body betrayed me.   _____

6. I can't protect myself.   _____

7. Sex is dirty.   _____

8. I have to be in control.   _____

9. I must be gay.   _____

10. I should have never told.   _____

A PICTURE IS WORTH A THOUSAND WORDS

GOALS OF THE EXERCISE

1.   For younger children to express their thoughts and feelings.
2.   To begin a process of healing.

ADDITIONAL HOMEWORK THAT MAY BE APPLICABLE TO CHILD SEXUAL ABUSE

• Adoption	My Safe Place	Page 14
• Anger Problems	Why Am I So Angry?	Page 18
• Anger Problems	Go Blow Out Some Candles	Page 27
• Depression	What Am I Thinking When I Am Feeling Depressed?	Page 104
• Suicide Attempts	Creating a Positive Outlook	Page 204

ADDITIONAL PROBLEMS FOR WHICH THIS EXERCISE MAY BE USEFUL

•   Domestic Violence*
•   Physical Abuse*

SUGGESTIONS FOR PROCESSING THIS EXERCISE WITH CLIENT

When treating younger children, oftentimes it is easier for them to draw their thoughts and feelings than to express them in words. Encourage parents to spend some time with their child who has been abused and ask him/her to draw pictures of the people and places listed in the following exercises. These pictures should then be shared with the therapist.

---

* These problems are not specifically discussed in detail in this volume.

A PICTURE IS WORTH A THOUSAND WORDS

FOR THE ABUSED CHILD'S PARENT(S) AND THE CHILD

Arrange for some special one-on-one time with your child and ask him or her to draw pictures of people and places listed on the following pages. These pictures should then be shared with the therapist.

1. Draw a picture of yourself.

2.   Draw a picture of a place that makes you feel safe and happy.

3.   Draw a picture of a person (or people) you trust and who makes you feel good.

4.   If you can, draw a picture of the person who abused you.

COMMUNICATION PROBLEMS

HOW CAN I TALK SO HE'LL LISTEN?

GOALS OF THE EXERCISE

1. To learn effective ways of communicating.
2. To feel acknowledged and heard.
3. To improve assertiveness and be able to convey your true thoughts and feelings.

ADDITIONAL HOMEWORK THAT MAY BE APPLICABLE TO COMMUNICATION PROBLEMS

- Depression   What Am I Thinking When I Am Depressed?   Page 104
- Intolerance/Defensiveness   Why Can't You Understand My Side for   Page 162
  Once?

ADDITIONAL PROBLEMS IN WHICH THIS EXERCISE MAY BE USEFUL

- Family Conflict*

SUGGESTIONS FOR PROCESSING THIS EXERCISE WITH CLIENT

It is very common in families experiencing conflict to have difficulties with communication. Members frequently report that they feel dismissed, unheard, and misunderstood. Unfortunately, there are not many places where people learn how to effectively communicate with each other. All of us are pretty much left to our experiences with others and watching how our parents, siblings, relatives, teachers, and friends communicate. A primary problem people have in communicating effectively is difficulties with listening. The following exercise is designed to help people learn in a step-by-step fashion how to listen actively and effectively as well as express their thoughts and feelings clearly and directly.

---

* This problem is not specifically discussed in detail in this volume.

HOW CAN I TALK SO HE'LL LISTEN?

FOR ALL FAMILY MEMBERS

In any communication process there must be a listener and a speaker. For communication to be effective, the individuals involved must learn when they are to be the speaker and when they are to be the listener. Therefore, the first step is having individuals take turns practicing being the speaker and the listener. Each person should practice assuming each role three to four times across several days. While practicing, keep the following guidelines in mind.

FOR THE LISTENER

1. Only make statements that paraphrase what you heard. Do not infer what you THINK the speaker meant or what she/he may have intended to say.

2. Use steady (but not necessarily constant) eye contact so that you convey visually to the speaker that you hear what he/she is saying.

3. Do not be involved in any other activity while listening to the speaker, no matter how insignificant you believe that activity is. Give your undivided attention to the speaker at all times.

4. Do not defend or explain your position until the speaker states that she/he believes you have heard and understood what was being said.

5. Don't interrupt: It's difficult to hear when you are talking yourself.

6. Clarify what you hear: Sum up or make clear your understanding of what is being said at the end of a statement or phrase. This will aid you in getting the correct message. It is also important to admit if you don't understand something.

7. Reflect on what you hear: This is different from clarification. Reflection involves showing your spouse that you are aware or understand what he/she feels. In essence, you hold up a mirror so your spouse can see what he or she is saying.

8. Summarizing: Both speaker and listener should always attempt to summarize their conversation so that no loose ends are remaining and both have a clear understanding of what has been discussed. A summary also allows a couple to set a direction for constructive follow-up.

FOR THE SPEAKER

1. Use "I" statements in describing your position/thoughts/feelings. Do not engage in accusing or blaming your listener.

2. Speak briefly (2 to 3 minutes at a time) and ask for the listener to repeat back to you what she/he heard. This is referred to as *reflective listening*.

3. If the listener is inaccurate with his/her reflections, repeat what you said. It is your responsibility to convey a clear message and to ensure that the message has been accurately received.

4. Speak attentively: Just as one listens attentively, one should also speak in the same manner, maintaining appropriate and direct eye contact and looking for body signals (facial or posture) that indicate the other person is listening.

5. Phrase meaningful questions: One way to keep a conversation short (and unproductive) is to ask a question that can be answered by either a "Yes" or a "No." Instead, try to ask questions that lead to more of a response from the other person that will help you understand him/her better.

6. Don't overtalk: Speak to the point and avoid drawn-out statements that "overtell" a story or reaction. This will give the other person a chance to clarify and reflect on what he or she hears from you.

7. Accept silence: Sometimes one of the best ways to make a point is to pause or use a period of silence after speaking. This allows both you and your listener to digest what is being said.

8. Don't cross-examine: Avoid firing questions at the other person when attempting to learn something during a conversation. The use of tact and diplomacy expresses respect and may serve as a far better means of learning what you need to know.

It is often helpful to practice these roles in the therapy session first and then at home. At home, family members should also videotape or audiotape the conversations for later review with their therapist.

EVERYTHING IS ALWAYS NEGATIVE IN OUR HOUSE

GOALS OF THE EXERCISE

1. To improve and increase the rate of positive verbal interactions between family members.
2. To create a more positive view of family life.
3. To improve family cohesion and increase the sense of engagement within the family unit.

ADDITIONAL HOMEWORK THAT MAY BE APPLICABLE TO COMMUNICATION PROBLEMS

- Depression   What Am I Thinking When I Am Depressed?   Page 104
- Intolerance/Defensiveness   Why Can't You Understand My Side for   Page 160
                                Once?

ADDITIONAL PROBLEMS FOR WHICH THIS EXERCISE MAY BE USEFUL

- Jealousy/Insecurity

SUGGESTIONS FOR PROCESSING THIS EXERCISE WITH CLIENT

Families experiencing difficulties with communication are often high in conflict and low in cohesiveness. Interactions tend to be more negative than positive. As a result, the number of interactions tends to decrease as members seek to avoid the conflicts that typically prevail. Thus in such a situation it is important for family members to increase the frequency of positive exchanges. This requires quite a bit of effort. At first, family members will feel that they are being insincere with one another. Explain that this is not unusual and should be expected at first. Let them know that sometimes changes in our beliefs and perceptions need to start with behavioral changes. The following exercise targets the behavior change needed to decrease the communication problems and conflicts.

EVERYTHING IS ALWAYS NEGATIVE IN OUR HOUSE

FOR ALL FAMILY MEMBERS

This exercise is designed for you and your family to find ways of focusing on and increasing the amount of positive interactions. Each family member should participate in this exercise. Each of you will need some index cards or paper to write on and a pen or pencil.

1. Each family member is to identify five (5) characteristics that he/she likes about himself/herself. This list of positive characteristics should then be shared with all family members.

2. Have each family member also list at least five (5) things that he/she would like others to do for him/her and share this list as well.

3. For at least three (3) days over the next week, each family member is to select another person's list out of a hat. That day he/she is to do at least one thing or say at least one thing from the list of the family member that he/she has selected.

Section XI

DEATH/LOSS ISSUES

GONE BUT NOT FORGOTTEN

GOALS OF THE EXERCISE

1. To describe your thoughts and feelings about the person who passed away.
2. To experience a healthy way to grieve/mourn.
3. To create a memory album that can serve as a keepsake.

ADDITIONAL HOMEWORK THAT MAY BE APPLICABLE TO DEATH/LOSS ISSUES

• Child Sexual Abuse	A Picture Is Worth a Thousand Words (just pictures 1–3)	Page 81
• Depression	What Am I Thinking When I Am Feeling Depressed?	Page 104
• Suicide Attempts	Creating a Positive Outlook	Page 204

ADDITIONAL PROBLEMS IN WHICH THIS EXERCISE MAY BE USEFUL

-   Adoption
-   Depression
-   Foster Care

SUGGESTIONS FOR PROCESSING THIS EXERCISE WITH CLIENT

Death of a loved one is always hard. Different people grieve in different ways and over different lengths of time. Sometimes this grief takes such a strong hold it is difficult to move on with one's life. Sometimes individuals feel that if they give up the feelings of grief they will be giving up the memory of their loved one. One way to let go of the feelings of grief without "forgetting" about your loved one is by creating a memory album. A memory album can be made up of pictures as well as words. Some find writing to be a positive and easy way to get things off of their chest. Sometimes, however, this process is difficult to get started. The following exercise provides a format to help a person write a letter and express his or her thoughts and feelings about the person who passed away.

GONE BUT NOT FORGOTTEN

Death of a loved one is always hard. Different people grieve in different ways and over different lengths of time. Sometimes this grief takes such a strong hold it is difficult to move on with one's life. Sometimes individuals feel that if they give up the feelings of grief they will be giving up the memory of their loved one. One way to let go of the feelings of grief without "forgetting" about your loved one is by creating a memory album. A memory album can be made up of pictures as well as words. Some find writing to be a positive and easy way to get things off of their chest. Sometimes, however, this process is difficult to get started. The following exercise provides a format to help you write a letter and express your thoughts and feelings about the person who passed away.

1. To start, make a title page for your memory album. You can color it or decorate it any way you want.

2. Inside the album describe your memories of _____ (person who passed away). Start with your earliest memory of him or her. You might want to draw this or find a Polaroid snapshot that describes your memory. Title the picture or drawing as well and put the date when memory occurred.

3. You can also use the following questions and sentence stems to write a letter expressing your thoughts and feelings. The letter or album can be an individual or a family project.

4. For the next several pages draw, write, or use a picture that describes times when:

   A. you were together with _____ (person who passed away)

   B. you were together with _____ (person who passed away) and the rest of your family

   C. you were doing something fun with _____ (person who passed away)

   D. you were upset or worried about _____ (person who passed away)

   E. you were angry at _____ (person who passed away)

   F. you admired _____ (person who passed away)

5. For each of the times just described, explain how you felt._____

_____

_____

_____

_____

_____

_____

_____

_____

6. Write, draw, or use a picture that describes a story you remember about
    _____ (person who passed away). _____

_____

_____

_____

_____

_____

_____

_____

7. Write, draw, or use a picture to describe the last thing you did with _____
    (person who passed away). Write and/or draw the feeling you had. _____

_____

_____

_____

_____

_____

_____

8. Write, draw, or use a picture to describe any unresolved feelings you have about
    _____ and how you would have wanted it to be resolved._____

_____

_____

_____

_____

_____

_____

9. Describe what _____ died from. _____

   _____

   _____

   _____

   _____

   _____

10. Write, draw, or use a picture to describe how you heard the news. Where were you
    and who told you?_____

    _____

    _____

    _____

    _____

    _____

    _____

    _____

11. Write, draw, or use a picture to describe what do you remember thinking and feeling
    when you heard the news._____

    _____

    _____

    _____

    _____

    _____

    _____

12. Write, draw, or use a picture to describe the memorial service/funeral. _____

    _____

    _____

    _____

    _____

    _____

    _____

    _____

13. Write, draw, or use a picture to describe three positive memories/images that you will never forget about _____. _____

   _____

   _____

   _____

   _____

   _____

   _____

   _____

14. Share each of the previous memories with other family members in a family meeting.

Section XII

DEPRESSION

SOMEONE IN MY FAMILY IS DEPRESSED

GOALS OF THE EXERCISE

1. Determine the family member's understanding about depression.
2. Identify how other family members feel affected by the family member with depression.
3. Identify triggers to the depression.
4. Develop ways to demonstrate affective support to the family member with depression.

ADDITIONAL HOMEWORK THAT MAY BE APPLICABLE TO DEPRESSION

• Adoption	My Safe Place	Page 14
• Anxiety	When I Feel Anxious It Is Like . . .	Page 32
• Child Sexual Abuse	A Picture Is Worth a Thousand Words (just pictures 1–3)	Page 81
• Suicide Attempts	Creating a Positive Outlook	Page 204

ADDITIONAL PROBLEMS IN WHICH THIS EXERCISE MAY BE USEFUL

- Anger
- Anxiety
- Behavioral Problems

SUGGESTIONS FOR PROCESSING THIS EXERCISE WITH CLIENT

This exercise is designed for all family members to complete and then to discuss, either in a family meeting or a family session.

SOMEONE IN MY FAMILY IS DEPRESSED

FOR EACH FAMILY MEMBER

This exercise is designed for all family members to complete and then discuss, either in a family meeting or a family session.

Define "depression": _____
_____

What does _____ do that tells me she/he is depressed? Try to identify at least four situations. _____

1.   He/she _____
    _____

    When he/she does this I think and feel _____
    _____

2.   He/she _____
    _____

    When he/she does this I think and feel _____
    _____

3.   He/she _____
    _____

    When he/she does this I think and feel _____
    _____

4.   He/she _____
    _____

    When he/she does this I think and feel _____
    _____

WHEN AM I DEPRESSED?

GOALS OF THE EXERCISE

1. Identify times and situations when/where an individual tends to feel depressed.
2. Increase an individual's ability to self-monitor.

ADDITIONAL HOMEWORK THAT MAY BE APPLICABLE TO DEPRESSION

• Adoption	My Safe Place	Page 14
• Anxiety	When I Feel Anxious It Is Like . . .	Page 32
• Child Sexual Abuse	A Picture Is Worth a Thousand Words (just pictures 1–3)	Page 81
• Suicide Attempts	Creating a Positive Outlook	Page 204

ADDITIONAL PROBLEMS IN WHICH THIS EXERCISE MAY BE USEFUL

- Addictions
- Anger
- Anxiety

SUGGESTIONS FOR PROCESSING THIS EXERCISE WITH CLIENT

This exercise is to help individuals identify and describe their experience of depression. It is designed to help individuals connect thoughts with feelings and behaviors. The more an individual is aware of his/her thoughts and behaviors with regard to his/her feelings, the more empowered that person may become to make changes.

WHEN AM I DEPRESSED?

This exercise will help you to identify and describe what you think about and do when you feel depressed. The more you are aware of your thoughts and behaviors with regard to your feelings, the more equipped you can be to make changes. Take some time during the next week and think about times you are feeling depressed or down. Complete the statements below during such times. If you do not feel comfortable sharing your responses with your family members right away, then bring this to your next therapy session.

FOR THE PARENT WHO IS DEPRESSED

List what you think when you feel depressed. This should be shared with all family members.

When I think _____ I feel depressed.

When I think _____ I feel depressed.

When I think _____ I feel depressed.

When I think _____ I feel depressed.

When I think _____ I feel depressed.

List what you do when you feel depressed. This should be shared with all family members.

When I do _____ I feel depressed.

When I do _____ I feel depressed.

When I do _____ I feel depressed.

When I do _____ I feel depressed.

When I do _____ I feel depressed.

I am not depressed when I think about _____

_____

I am not depressed when I think about _____

_____

I am not depressed when I am doing _____

_____

I am not depressed when I am doing _____

_____

WHAT AM I THINKING WHEN I AM FEELING DEPRESSED?

GOALS OF THE EXERCISE

1. Identify the various thoughts that go through an individual's mind when feeling depressed.
2. Identify possible triggers to the depression.

ADDITIONAL HOMEWORK THAT MAY BE APPLICABLE TO DEPRESSION

• Adoption	My Safe Place	Page 14
• Anxiety	When I Feel Anxious It Is Like . . .	Page 32
• Child Sexual Abuse	A Picture Is Worth a Thousand Words (just pictures 1–3)	Page 81
• Suicide Attempts	Creating a Positive Outlook	Page 204

ADDITIONAL PROBLEMS FOR WHICH THIS EXERCISE MAY BE USEFUL

- Addictions
- Anger
- Anxiety
- Communication Problems
- Eating Disorders

SUGGESTIONS FOR PROCESSING THIS EXERCISE WITH CLIENT

Have all family members choose the cognitive distortions they tend to engage in, and have them give an example of each one. (See the exercise "My/Our Daughter Is Depressed" (pages 109–110) for a list of common cognitive distortions.)

WHAT AM I THINKING WHEN
I AM FEELING DEPRESSED?

FOR ALL FAMILY MEMBERS

At times, our thoughts can greatly influence how we feel. One of the first steps to changing how we feel is to identify how we think. By completing this exercise, you will learn how you sometimes think and perceive things.

This week I _____

_____

This was an example of the following cognitive distortion _____

This week I _____

_____

This was an example of the following cognitive distortion _____

This week I _____

_____

This was an example of the following cognitive distortion _____

WHAT DO OTHERS VALUE ABOUT ME?

GOALS OF THE EXERCISE

1.   To develop a sense of value.
2.   To develop a stronger sense of self-worth.

ADDITIONAL HOMEWORK THAT MAY BE APPLICABLE TO DEPRESSION

ADDITIONAL PROBLEMS IN WHICH THIS EXERCISE MAY BE USEFUL

*   Anger
*   Anxiety

SUGGESTIONS FOR PROCESSING THIS EXERCISE WITH CLIENT

Many individuals who suffer from depression report feeling a lack of value. To counter such negative thinking, have them complete the exercise on the following page.

WHAT DO OTHERS VALUE ABOUT ME?

This exercise is designed to help you challenge your belief or view of how valued you are by others.

Seek out at least two family members and two friends, and ask them, "What do you value about me?" Record their responses verbatim.

1. _____ said that she/he values me because _____
   _____

2. _____ said that she/he values me because _____
   _____

3. _____ said that she/he values me because _____
   _____

4. _____ said that she/he values me because _____
   _____

Share the findings with some other family members, then have those family members record times when they observe the evidence of this value (i.e., you are thoughtful, you helped Johnny with his homework).

MY/OUR DAUGHTER IS DEPRESSED

GOALS OF THE EXERCISE

1. Help the depressed adolescent identify various thinking errors (distorted thoughts) that lead to depression.
2. Begin to generate a sense of control over feeling depressed.

ADDITIONAL HOMEWORK THAT MAY BE APPLICABLE TO DEPRESSION

- Adoption   My Safe Place   Page 14
- Anxiety   When I Feel Anxious It Is Like . . .   Page 32
- Child Sexual Abuse   A Picture Is Worth a Thousand Words (just pictures 1–3)   Page 81
- Suicide Attempts   Creating a Positive Outlook   Page 204

ADDITIONAL PROBLEMS IN WHICH THIS EXERCISE MAY BE USEFUL

- Addictions
- Anger
- Anxiety
- Communication Problems

SUGGESTIONS FOR PROCESSING THIS EXERCISE WITH CLIENT

This exercise is a fun way for family members to become familiar with the various types of cognitive distortions that individuals sometimes engage in. At times, our thoughts can influence how we feel and perceive situations. This exercise is designed to help family members become more aware of cognitive distortions and to begin to aid them in identifying which distortions they tend to engage in.

MY/OUR DAUGHTER IS DEPRESSED

FOR ALL FAMILY MEMBERS

This exercise is a fun way for family members to become familiar with the various types of cognitive distortions that individuals sometimes engage in. At times, our thoughts can influence how we feel and perceive situations. This exercise is designed to help you become more aware of cognitive distortions and to identify ones you may engage in.

After reading the definition and example for each of the following thinking errors that many people make, see if you can find them in the word search on page 110.

- *Catastrophizing.* This is when you think about consequences and you blow them out of proportion in a negative way. For example, after striking out at bat, Joe says to himself, "I'll never get a hit. The coach will probably cut me from the team now. I'll never be able to play baseball again."
- *Overgeneralization.* This is when you think of one example to make conclusions about a number of other things, or all similar circumstances. For example, Tim breaks up with his girlfriend Becky, and Becky thinks to herself, "Guys are scum, and Tim is just like all the rest of them."
- *Fortune telling.* This is when you predict that negative things will happen to you in the future, based on little or no supporting evidence. For example, T.J. wants to play basketball for his school but begins to think, "They won't want me to play, I won't be as good as the other kids."
- *Black-and-white thinking.* This is when you look at situations, others, or even yourself as being totally bad or totally good—without any sense of balance. For example, Susan is thinking about her parents getting on her case about her school-work and she concludes, "I can never come home without having them get on my case. Every day it's the same thing."
- *Dark glasses or mental filtering.* This is when you block out all the positives and just focus on the negatives. For example, Mike brings home all As and Bs on his report card—except for one D. He thinks to himself repeatedly, "I am so dumb I can't even get better than a D."
- *Personalizing.* This is when you take on the responsibility for something that is not your job. For example, Sondra arranges to have pizza delivered to her house for a party she is having. The delivery person gets lost and never arrives with the pizza. She thinks to herself, "I should have never called that place. Why couldn't I have called the other pizza store?"

- *Discounting.* This is when you reject the positive things that happen to you. For example, Michelle's girlfriend tells Michelle that her outfit looks great, but Michelle thinks to herself, "This outfit looks terrible on me. She is just trying to say something nice but doesn't really mean it."

- *Judging.* This is when you are critical of yourself or others and make statements such as, "I should be more relaxed," "I ought to know by now," "I have to get this right."

- *Mind reading.* This is when you make a negative assumption regarding other people's thoughts and behaviors. For example, Bryan passes a girl in the hall and when she does not say hello to him he thinks, "She hates me. I don't stand a chance with her."

C	A	T	A	S	T	R	O	P	H	I	Z	I	N	G	B
M	D	F	O	S	R	F	G	H	J	K	B	L	F	B	L
I	A	F	V	J	K	L	W	Z	Y	B	J	S	O	J	A
N	W	G	R	Y	T	I	T	A	P	Q	G	H	R	K	C
D	O	F	R	Q	S	C	G	H	J	K	N	M	T	T	K
J	U	D	G	I	N	G	U	H	Q	S	D	D	U	R	W
P	M	U	E	E	A	F	J	I	V	S	F	A	N	A	H
A	G	G	N	I	Z	I	L	A	N	O	S	R	E	P	I
D	G	W	A	K	R	K	O	D	W	V	K	K	T	O	T
Q	K	O	R	U	G	Y	N	F	D	E	B	G	L	W	E
L	K	U	L	V	S	J	W	N	C	U	O	L	L	N	T
Q	W	G	I	L	T	E	R	I	N	G	K	A	L	W	H
K	U	H	Z	G	N	I	T	N	U	O	C	S	I	D	I
L	C	Z	I	B	T	D	J	N	K	S	V	S	N	N	N
K	M	I	N	D	R	E	A	D	I	N	G	E	G	P	K
S	Q	G	G	H	E	A	X	C	K	T	D	S	M	L	I
S	E	L	F	B	L	A	M	I	N	G	D	F	N	J	N
Q	F	S	O	L	B	N	G	K	J	X	G	E	J	K	G

Section XIII

DISILLUSIONMENT WITH FAMILY TIES

CIRCLES OF PERCEPTION

GOALS OF THE EXERCISE

1. To solicit family members' perception of their relationships to one another, particularly in those who have difficulty with verbal expression.
2. To implement an activity that will facilitate individual work, followed by an in-session collaboration.
3. To exchange ideas and perceptions of each other and broaden family members' conceptualizations of how they view themselves.

ADDITIONAL HOMEWORK THAT MAY BE APPLICABLE TO DISILLUSIONMENT WITH FAMILY TIES

• Depression   What Am I Thinking When I Am Feeling Depressed? Page 104

ADDITIONAL PROBLEMS IN WHICH THIS EXERCISE MAY BE USEFUL

• Anger Problems
• Communication Problems
• Dependency
• Disengagement
• Jealousy/Insecurity

SUGGESTIONS FOR PROCESSING THIS EXERCISE WITH CLIENT

Weekes and Treat (1992) first introduced the use of circles as a strategy in their work with couples. It was later expounded on by Dattilio (2000) who also applied it to couples and later to his work with families (Dattilio, 1997; 2001). This technique can be used in session, however, with families it may be more effective as a task assignment, particularly with younger children who may want to elaborate on their schematic diagrams with crayons or colored pens.

CIRCLES OF PERCEPTION

Trying to express in words how we see things can be difficult. This is especially true when it pertains to families and family members.

Sometimes, a simpler way to do this is to express what we see and how we feel through creative visual designs. Sometimes, the simpler the drawing, the better we are able to get our point across. This exercise is to help you express your perception of your family as you view it currently and how you would like it to be in the future. Try to be as honest as you can when constructing both drawings. Try not to worry too much about how the other family members may view your designs.

1. Take a clean piece of white paper (unlined). You can use a regular graphite pencil, colored pencils, or even crayons or colored ink pens. Using only one circle to represent each family member, draw how you view your family constellation as it exists. The closer the circles are, the more it indicates how emotionally close you feel that family members are. So, for example, your drawing may look similar to any of the following designs.

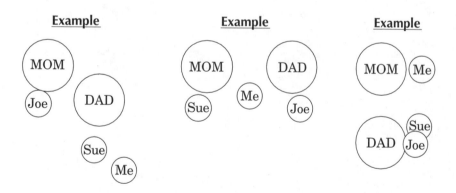

The large circles represent the parents or grandparents (adults) and the smaller circles represent the children.

After you have completed your drawing, take the other plain piece of paper, marking it Number 2. Using the same type of circles, draw how you would like to see your family ideally.

Bring both of your drawings to the next session and be prepared to discuss the following:

1.   Explain your drawings.

2.   How did you feel about doing this exercise?

3.   Did it make you think more about how your family members relate to one another?

4.   Did you find the task difficult to do?

5.   Did you notice a big difference between your first drawing and the second drawing?

6.   In what ways did your drawings differ from those of other family members?

The large circles represent the parents or grandparents (adults) and the smaller circles represent the children.

   After you have completed your drawing, take the other plain piece of paper, marking it #2 and using the same type of circles, draw how you would like to see your family ideally.

   Keep both of your drawings and be prepared to discuss them in the next session.

Section XIV

DIVORCE/SEPARATION

MY PARENTS ARE GETTING A DIVORCE

GOALS OF THE EXERCISE

1. Each member of the family expresses his or her fears about the family breakup. "We're no longer the family I knew," "I'll lose my mom/dad/brother/sister."
2. Help each family member define his or her role within the family. "Where do I fit in now that things have changed?"
3. Help family members identify when limits or boundaries are being broken.
4. Discuss the fears that children may have about their parents finding new spouses or moving the family to another location.

ADDITIONAL HOMEWORK THAT MAY BE APPLICABLE TO DIVORCE/SEPARATION

• Adoption	My Safe Place	Page 14
• Child Sexual Abuse	A Picture Is Worth a Thousand Words (just pictures 1–3)	Page 81
• Suicide Attempts	Creating a Positive Outlook	Page 204

ADDITIONAL PROBLEMS IN WHICH THIS EXERCISE MAY BE USEFUL

- Blended Families
- Death/Loss Issues
- Foster Care
- Geographic Relocation

SUGGESTIONS FOR PROCESSING THIS EXERCISE WITH CLIENT

This exercise is designed to help teens and preteens express their thoughts and feelings regarding their parents' separation or divorce.

ONE MORE IDEA

Suggest the use of certain reading materials, such as:

- *Dinosaur's Divorce* (for children under 10) (Brown & Brown, 1998)
- *Children Are Not Divorceable* (Bonkowski, 1990a)
- *Teens Are Not Divorceable* (Bonkowski, 1990b)

MY PARENTS ARE GETTING A DIVORCE

FOR TEENS/PRETEENS WHOSE PARENTS ARE DIVORCING

Write a letter, using the following questions and incomplete sentence blanks, to describe your thoughts and feelings regarding your parents' separation and how things might be after (or now that) they have separated.

1. I think my parents should not be separated because: _____
    _____
    _____

2. I think they should be separated because: _____
    _____
    _____

3. Describe at least one thing you remember that you like and at least one thing that you do not care for about each family member. _____
    _____
    _____
    _____

4. What I remember most about my family as a whole (before my parents decided to separate) was: _____
    _____
    _____

5. The worst thing about my parents getting a divorce or being separated is: _____
    _____
    _____
    _____

6. One of the things I notice that is different about my family now that my parents are separated (or now that my parents have told me that they plan to get a divorce) is:
    _____
    _____
    _____

7.   What I like about the way things are now is: _____

_____

_____

_____

8.   What I do not like about the way things are now is: _____

_____

_____

_____

EATING DISORDERS

I NEED TO GET CONTROL

GOALS OF THE EXERCISE

1. To gain some control over the frequency of eating/dieting/weight-controlling behaviors.
2. To get a sense of how often these behaviors are occurring.

ADDITIONAL HOMEWORK THAT MAY BE APPLICABLE TO EATING DISORDERS

ADDITIONAL PROBLEMS IN WHICH THIS EXERCISE MAY BE USEFUL

*   Addictions
*   Anger

SUGGESTIONS FOR PROCESSING THIS EXERCISE WITH CLIENT

Many adolescents, especially females, are at risk of developing some kind of eating disorder. The heavy emphasis in our society to be thin reinforces the idea of having a slender and well-defined body. This need to fit into society's expectations can quickly get out of control and become an obsession. Some of the most effective treatment interventions have relied on the use of linking one's thoughts and behaviors. As a result, the following exercise utilizes this cognitive-behavioral approach.

I NEED TO GET CONTROL

FOR THE ADOLESCENT EXPERIENCING AN EATING DISORDER

1. On the charts provided record the times that you engage in any kind of eating/dieting/weight control behavior (i.e., not eating a meal, purging).
2. Describe how you are feeling before, during, and after this behavior.
3. Describe what you are thinking before, during, and after this behavior.

Behavior		Thought	Feeling	Day	Time
	Before				
	During				
	After				

Behavior		Thought	Feeling	Day	Time
	Before				
	During				
	After				

Behavior		Thought	Feeling	Day	Time
	Before				
	During				
	After				

Behavior		Thought	Feeling	Day	Time
	Before				
	During				
	After				

WHAT AM I THINKING?

GOALS OF THE EXERCISE

1. To identify the types of thinking errors the individual engages in.
2. To identify the feeling you have when you think such thoughts.
3. To generate more adaptive/realistic self-talk and identify alternative responses.
4. Describe the feeling you have when you think about the alternative statement.

ADDITIONAL HOMEWORK THAT MAY BE APPLICABLE TO EATING DISORDERS

ADDITIONAL PROBLEMS FOR WHICH THIS EXERCISE MAY BE USEFUL

- Addictions
- Anger
- Anxiety
- Depression

SUGGESTIONS FOR PROCESSING THIS EXERCISE WITH CLIENT

Individuals with an eating disorder are constantly in their heads and engage in various types of cognitive distortions. They may think that if they start eating they won't be able to stop. They may believe that the only way to "look good" is to exercise and not eat. Such thoughts are generally based in some kind of fear (i.e., of becoming overweight, losing control, being rejected). It is important for these individuals to get such thoughts and fears out of their head and to externalize them. To begin this process of overcoming and letting go of such powerful and overwhelming thinking, first review the list of common cognitive distortions that follows. Once you and your client have discussed some examples of each distortion and how your client engages in such thinking and how he/she can restructure such thoughts, have him/her fill in the charts in the accompanying exercise.

Dichotomous Thinking—Experiences are codified as either all or nothing (e.g., "I am either fat or not, there's no in-between").

Tunnel Vision—Seeing what fits one's current state of mind (e.g., "If I eat only foods with starch, I'll get fat and won't be able to lose the weight").

Mind Reading—Assuming what others are thinking without the benefit of verbal communication (e.g., "I know that when people look at me, they think that I am too fat").

Arbitrary Inference—Conclusions are made in the absence of substantiating evidence (e.g., "If I am not a perfect body weight, no one will like me").

Catastrophizing—This is when you think about consequences and you blow them out of proportion in a negative way. For example, you are counting points for a Weight Watchers program or calories for the day and you exceed your allotted number. You respond by thinking, "I can't believe I did that. I might as well give up now because I can never stick to anything."

Dark Glasses or Mental Filtering—This is when you block out the positives and just focus on the negatives. For example, two of your friends meet you at the mall. One friend remarks about how good you look. You begin to think that your other friend must believe you to look pretty awful.

Discounting—This is when you reject the positive things that happen to you. For example, over a week's time, you refrain from purging for four days. Instead of looking at the positive, you think, "I am so weak, I purged on three days this past week."

WHAT AM I THINKING?

FOR THE PERSON EXPERIENCING AN EATING DISORDER

This exercise is designed to help you begin the process of getting control over your behaviors, thoughts, and feelings about eating, body weight, or body shape. Use the list of cognitive distortions from your personal experience that you discussed with your therapist to complete the following charts.

Behavior	Thought	Type of Distortion	Feeling

Alternative Thought	Feeling

WHY IS SHE DOING THIS?

GOALS OF THE EXERCISE

1. To allow each family member a chance to express his/her feelings regarding living with a family member with an eating disorder.
2. To help the therapist understand each family member's conceptualization of eating disorders.

ADDITIONAL HOMEWORK THAT MAY BE APPLICABLE TO EATING DISORDERS

• Addictions	Staying Clean	Page 2
• Addictions	What Else Can I Do?	Page 5
• Adoption	My Safe Place	Page 14
• Child Sexual Abuse	A Picture Is Worth a Thousand Words (just pictures 1–3)	Page 81
• Depression	What Am I Thinking When I Am Feeling Depressed?	Page 104
• Depression	What Do Others Value about Me?	Page 106
• Suicide Attempts	Creating a Positive Outlook	Page 204

ADDITIONAL PROBLEMS IN WHICH THIS EXERCISE MAY BE USEFUL

- Addictions
- Anger
- Anxiety
- Depression

SUGGESTIONS FOR PROCESSING THIS EXERCISE WITH CLIENT

Family members may not have an accurate understanding of what the "problem" is regarding a family member who has an eating disorder. Learning what each family member perceives to be the problem and his/her feelings regarding this is important for the therapist to know in order to develop treatment plans.

WHY IS SHE DOING THIS?

FOR INDIVIDUALS WHO HAVE A FAMILY MEMBER WITH AN EATING DISORDER

The following exercise will help you construct your perception and understanding of an eating disorder. It will also help you identify how you feel about the situation and how to deal with the family member who has this problem.

1. Describe what an eating disorder is from your perspective. _____
    _____
    _____
    _____
    _____

2. What do you see or hear that makes you believe _____ has an eating disorder? _____
    _____
    _____
    _____

3. When you see _____ engaging in eating-disordered-like behavior, how does that make you feel? _____
    _____
    _____

4. What do you wish you could do? _____
    _____
    _____
    _____

5. How does _____ respond to you when you try to help? _____
    _____
    _____
    _____
    _____

6. How does that make you feel? _____
   _____
   _____

7. How could you be a support to _____? _____
   _____
   _____
   _____

Section XVI

EXTERNAL ACTIVITIES AFFECTING FAMILY ROLE

WHEN CAN WE BE TOGETHER?

GOALS OF THE EXERCISE

1. To find an acceptable balance between the competing demands of external activities and family responsibilities.
2. Reduce family tension/stress related to lack of family time

ADDITIONAL HOMEWORK THAT MAY BE APPLICABLE TO EXTERNAL ACTIVITIES AFFECTING FAMILY ROLE

• Behavioral Problems in Children and Adolescents	Acting As If	Page 42
• Communication Problems	Everything Is Always Negative in Our House	Page 90
• Intolerance/Defensiveness	Why Can't You Understand My Side for Once?	Page 160

ADDITIONAL PROBLEMS IN WHICH THIS EXERCISE MAY BE USEFUL

- Anger Problems
- Communication Problems
- Disengagement*
- Jealousy/Insecurity

SUGGESTIONS FOR PROCESSING THIS EXERCISE WITH CLIENT

Many families have difficulty finding time for each other. Children are often involved in numerous activities, and frequently both parents are working. As a result, family time is competing with a multitude of other activities and demands. The following exercise is designed to help family members create time for the family as a whole.

---

* This problem is not specifically discussed in detail in this volume.

WHEN CAN WE BE TOGETHER?

FOR ALL FAMILY MEMBERS

The following exercise is designed to help family members create time for the family as a whole. Each of you will need some paper and a pen or pencil. During a family meeting, respond to the following statements:

1. Each family member is to express his/her priorities regarding how time is spent (e.g., family time, work, individual time, friends etc.).

2. Each family member is to then rank in order these priorities, from the most important to the least important.

3. Estimate how much time is currently being spent on each priority.

4. Each family member is to express his/her feelings regarding the lack of time spent together as a family or with a particular family member.

5. Each family member is to describe how much time he/she would like to spend as a family or with a particular family member.

6. As a family, brainstorm a list of possible family activities (i.e., monthly family night out or night in, weekly family meetings to touch base with others and share how his/her week has been, monthly lunch date with dad, monthly shopping trip with mom).

7. Get a calendar and as a family pick some specific dates and activities that you will share together as a family.

Section XVII

FAMILY BUSINESS CONFLICTS

A CHANGING OF THE GUARD

GOALS OF THE EXERCISE

1. Achieve some boundaries regarding who is in charge of a family business.
2. Resolve issues of ownership and power in a family business.
3. Formalize the transition of a new generation carrying on the family business.

ADDITIONAL HOMEWORK THAT MAY BE APPLICABLE TO FAMILY BUSINESS CONFLICTS

ADDITIONAL PROBLEMS FOR WHICH THIS EXERCISE MAY BE USEFUL

- Blended Families
- Disengagement*

SUGGESTIONS FOR PROCESSING THIS EXERCISE WITH CLIENT

A family business has many positives, but there can also be some awkward and uncomfortable times. This is especially true when the next generation is given the reins and expected to run the business. Sometimes those who have been in charge have difficulty giving up their control, and still want the final say. It is important for family members to discuss and come to terms regarding who has what role and what that role means. As a way to signify the changing of the guard, so to speak, it is oftentimes beneficial to have a ceremony.

---

* This problem is not specifically discussed in detail in this volume.

A CHANGING OF THE GUARD

The following exercise is designed to help those family members who are currently in charge to hand over the reins to the new leaders or bosses.

1. Have those family members who are currently "in charge" purchase or design a big key, to symbolize the keys to the business.

2. Have the family then go out to dinner and have the current members in charge make a speech announcing the names of the family members who will from this time forward (or starting on a specific date) be the new "bosses."

3. At the end of the speech present the key to the new bosses.

WHO IS DOING WHAT?

GOALS OF THE EXERCISE

1. Establish guidelines for boundaries and define roles of each family member in a family business.
2. Achieve agreement regarding the levels of power and responsibilities among family members in a family business.

ADDITIONAL HOMEWORK THAT MAY BE APPLICABLE TO FAMILY BUSINESS CONFLICTS

- Intolerance/Defensiveness   Why Can't You Understand My Side   Page 160
  for Once?

ADDITIONAL PROBLEMS FOR WHICH THIS EXERCISE MAY BE USEFUL

- Blended Families
- Family Conflicts around House Chores*

SUGGESTIONS FOR PROCESSING THIS EXERCISE WITH CLIENT

Once a changing of the guard in a family business is official, family members still need to identify who is responsible for what aspects of the business. One area of conflict that frequently arises during such transitions involves how things have been conducted in the past and the way in which the next generation want things to work. Another salient issue has to do with the amount of say and control those who have turned over the keys still maintain.

---

* This problem is not specifically discussed in detail in this volume.

WHO IS DOING WHAT?

FOR FAMILY MEMBERS INVOLVED IN A FAMILY BUSINESS

The following exercise will help you to establish guidelines for boundaries and define roles of each member in the family business. Each person involved should read and respond to the first two items by him/herself.

1. Have family members identify their skills and strengths. (This can be used for a family discussion in the next session.)

2. Have family members put in writing the needs of the business. It would be helpful to have those who were most recently in charge, as well as those who have just transitioned into that role, to identify the goals/objectives of the business for the coming year.

3. Have the family meet as a group and match the skills/strengths of each family member to the various roles and responsibilities within the business.

Section XVIII

FAMILY-OF-ORIGIN INTERFERENCE

THANKS, BUT NO THANKS

GOALS OF THE EXERCISE

1. Reduce the marital and family conflict regarding family-of-origin interference with family issues.
2. Identify the thoughts and feelings associated with the interferences.

ADDITIONAL HOMEWORK THAT MAY BE APPLICABLE TO FAMILY-OF-ORIGIN INTERFERENCE

ADDITIONAL PROBLEMS FOR WHICH THIS EXERCISE MAY BE USEFUL

- Communication Problems
- Jealousy/Insecurity

SUGGESTIONS FOR PROCESSING THIS EXERCISE WITH CLIENT

The well-meaning intentions of parents, grandparents, and other family-of-origin members can at times become very destructive forces—especially when such input is unwelcome or uninvited. The marital dyad will frequently argue over their spouse's family of origin stepping over the boundary lines. Children/adolescents will also begin to act out emotionally and behaviorally as the result of such interference. Therefore, the couple and their children/adolescents need to find a way to establish boundaries. Another key is developing a sense of cohesion as a family.

THANKS, BUT NO THANKS

FOR THE COUPLE EXPERIENCING FAMILY-OF-ORIGIN INTERFERENCE WITH FAMILY ISSUES

The following exercise is designed to help you gain a clearer perspective of your concerns as a couple regarding the involvement of other family members in your family issues. You will need paper and pen to record some lists. Find some quiet time, in which the two of you can complete, the following:

1. As a couple, identify your perceptions of the interfacing by other family members. You can do this individually first and then compare your lists.

2. Once the perceptions are identified, designate the accompanying feelings by using "I" statements.

3. As a couple, practice effective communication skills and active listening. (See the homework on Communication Problems, pages 88–91.)

HOW CAN I TELL HER TO MIND HER OWN BUSINESS?

GOALS OF THE EXERCISE

1. Establish boundaries and limits regarding the roles of family-of-origin family members.
2. Develop assertiveness skills.
3. Develop a sense of support and cohesion, especially within the marital dyad.

ADDITIONAL HOMEWORK THAT MAY BE APPLICABLE TO FAMILY-OF-ORIGIN INTERFERENCE

• Behavioral Problems in Children and Adolescents	Acting As If	Page 42
• Communication Problems	How Can I Talk So He'll Listen?	Page 87
• Intolerance/Defensiveness	Why Can't You Understand My Side for Once?	Page 160
• Jealousy/Insecurity	I Am Not Jealous	Page 165

ADDITIONAL PROBLEMS FOR WHICH THIS EXERCISE MAY BE USEFUL

• Communication Problems
• Jealousy/Insecurity

SUGGESTIONS FOR PROCESSING THIS EXERCISE WITH CLIENT

When members of the family-of-origin interfere, the most frequent emotional reaction is frustration and anger. Oftentimes this frustration and anger compounds, only later to become unleashed onto others unintentionally. Because such feelings can lead to resentments and conflict within the marital relationship, it is important that couples establish ways to remain unified and supportive of each other.

HOW CAN I TELL HER TO MIND HER OWN BUSINESS?

FOR THE COUPLE EXPERIENCING FAMILY-OF-ORIGIN INTERFERENCE WITH FAMILY ISSUES

When members of a family-of-origin interfere, the most frequent emotional reaction is frustration and anger. Oftentimes this frustration and anger compounds, only later to become unleashed onto others unintentionally. The following exercise is designed to help you as a couple to establish ways to stay unified and supportive to each other.

1. For the next week, make daily comments to your partner regarding how much you appreciate and care about him/her.

2. Individually, or as a couple, identify a list of situations in which family-of-origin members interfere.

3. At least three times over the next week, set aside quiet and alone time to express your concerns (using "I" statements) to each other, regarding the interference by family-of-origin family members.

4. During this quiet and alone time (and preferably after having practiced in a therapy session), use role-playing techniques in front of each other to practice being assertive to an interfering family-of-origin family member.

5. Prior to situations with family-of-origin family members who tend to interfere, review the previous role-play.

Section XIX

FOSTER CARE

I WANT TO GO HOME

GOALS OF THE EXERCISE

1. Identify thoughts and feelings about placement.
2. Recognize and acknowledge desire for reunification.
3. Develop action plan to achieve reunification.

ADDITIONAL HOMEWORK THAT MAY BE APPLICABLE TO FOSTER CARE

- Adoption — My Safe Place — Page 14
- Child Sexual Abuse — A Picture Is Worth a Thousand Words (just pictures 1–3) — Page 81
- Suicide Attempts — Creating a Positive Outlook — Page 204

ADDITIONAL PROBLEMS IN WHICH THIS EXERCISE MAY BE USEFUL

- Adoption
- Blended Families

SUGGESTIONS FOR PROCESSING THIS EXERCISE WITH CLIENT

Foster care placement occurs for a variety of reasons. The following exercise can be used with families in which the goal is for reunification of children with family members. It is designed for children and their parent(s) or legal guardian whom they will be reunited with once out of foster care.

I WANT TO GO HOME

This exercise is designed for families who are planning to reunite after experiencing foster care placement. The first part is only for the teens and preteens who have been in placement. The second part is for the family as a group to complete. The last part is for each member to complete individually and then to be shared with the family as a whole.

FOR THE TEEN/PRETEEN IN FOSTER CARE TO COMPLETE

When I was placed in foster care the reason was _____
_____
_____

My first night I felt _____ because _____
_____

Now I feel _____ about being in foster care.

I (circle) want to/do not want to be taken out of foster care and placed with _____
_____

FOR ALL FAMILY MEMBERS TO COMPLETE

List the pros and cons to being reunited.

Pros	Cons
_____	_____
_____	_____
_____	_____
_____	_____
_____	_____

FOR EACH INDIVIDUAL TO COMPLETE ABOUT HIMSELF OR HERSELF

In order for me to be united with _____

I need to do the following:

1. _____
2. _____

   _____

   _____

ONE MORE IDEA

1. Identify some older adults who may have experienced foster care during their youth. Ask them if they feel that the foster care has helped them in their new life.

Section XX

GEOGRAPHIC RELOCATION

WE'RE MOVING

GOALS OF THE EXERCISE

1. Identify and express feelings regarding relocation.
2. Family members be able to feel as though they have a voice in the decision.
3. Identify any alternative solutions to the relocation conflict.
4. Be able to cope effectively with the loss of friends and familiar environment.

ADDITIONAL HOMEWORK THAT MAY BE APPLICABLE TO RELOCATING

- Adoption   My Safe Place   Page 14
- External Activities Affecting Family Role   When Can We Be Together?   Page 131

ADDITIONAL PROBLEMS FOR WHICH THIS EXERCISE MAY BE USEFUL

- Blended Families

SUGGESTIONS FOR PROCESSING THIS EXERCISE WITH CLIENT

When a family is forced to relocate due to a parent's job, tremendous emotions usually emerge. This is especially true if family members are well-grounded (have roots) in their current community. Children—and particularly teenagers—can become quite oppositional to leaving their friends and familiar surroundings, and/or experience anxiety and depression.

One exercise that can be helpful is to instruct family members to identify and bring to the next session an object that is representative of the loss they fear about moving (i.e., student ID badge that might represent a teenager's identity). Each person must think about and describe what his/her fear is. The therapist is then able to address the fears and help each member be heard and their fear validated. The therapist can then help the family identify which things are negotiable and how such losses can be saved.

WE'RE MOVING

FOR ALL MEMBERS OF A FAMILY THAT IS EXPERIENCING RELOCATION

The following exercise can help each of you talk about the loss and associated feelings regarding having to move. Before your next session, identify an object that is representative of the loss you fear about relocating (e.g., student ID badge that might represent a teenager's identity). Each of you must think about and describe your fear. Be prepared to discuss this in the next family session. Be sure to bring in your object.

The object I brought is _____ . This represents my fear of _____

_____

_____

SHOULD WE OR SHOULD WE NOT?

GOALS OF THE EXERCISE

1. Have family identify the pros and cons of relocation.
2. Family members be able to feel as though they have a voice in the matter.
3. The family should consider possible alternatives to relocating.

ADDITIONAL HOMEWORK THAT MAY BE APPLICABLE TO RELOCATING

*   Adoption
*   External Activities Affecting Family Role
*   Suicide Attempts

ADDITIONAL PROBLEMS FOR WHICH THIS EXERCISE MAY BE USEFUL

*   Blended Families
*   Family Conflict

SUGGESTIONS FOR PROCESSING THIS EXERCISE WITH CLIENT

Oftentimes, relocating creates mixed feelings by all family members. When this occurs, family members frequently report feeling unheard. This exercise will help each family member identify his/her reasons for wanting to relocate or wanting to remain in their present domicile.

SHOULD WE OR SHOULD WE NOT?

FOR ALL MEMBERS OF A FAMILY THAT IS CONSIDERING RELOCATION

Relocating can be an overwhelming experience. It can create many mixed emotions. The following exercise is designed to help you sort out your thoughts and feelings and to listen to everyone else's as well.

1. As a family record a list of the advantages and the disadvantages for moving.

Pros	Cons
_____	_____
_____	_____
_____	_____
_____	_____
_____	_____
_____	_____

It is important to look at any alternatives to moving, but in fairness, all family members should also convey their understanding as to why other family members view the move as necessary. To achieve these two important aspects, family members should complete the following exercise.

2. The family members who think we should move are: _____

_____   _____

_____   _____

3. List each person who thinks you should move and his/her reason.

_____ reason for moving is _____

_____

_____ reason for moving is _____

_____

_____ reason for moving is _____

_____

_____ reason for moving is _____

_____

4. The family members who think we should NOT move are: _____

    _____   _____

    _____   _____

5. List each person who thinks you should NOT move and his/her reason. _____
    _____ reason for NOT moving is _____

    _____

    _____ reason for NOT moving is _____

    _____

    _____ reason for NOT moving is _____

    _____

6. I propose the following alternatives to moving: _____
    A. _____

    _____

    B. _____

    _____

    C. _____

    _____

ONE MORE IDEA

1. Suppose you had a best friend who came to you and informed you that they had to
    relocate to another area and had no choice in the matter. How would you recommend
    that they cope with the situation? What would your advice be to them? _____

    _____

    _____

2. Identify a classmate at your present school, or a neighbor who has relocated from
    another area at school. Talk to them about the difficulty they experienced and how
    long it took before they eventually settled into this new environment. _____

    _____

    _____

Section XXI

INHERITANCE DISPUTES

HE ALWAYS DID LIKE YOU BEST

GOALS OF THE EXERCISE

1. For family members to develop a sense of acceptance and understanding regarding the distribution of the will.
2. Resolve any disputes or resentments regarding the distribution of the inheritance.

ADDITIONAL HOMEWORK THAT MAY BE APPLICABLE TO INHERITANCE DISPUTES

ADDITIONAL PROBLEMS IN WHICH THIS EXERCISE MAY BE USEFUL

*   Divorce Situations*

SUGGESTIONS FOR PROCESSING THIS EXERCISE WITH CLIENT

The passing of a family member is typically hard no matter what the situation. Sometimes a complicating factor involves the distribution of the money and assets left behind. When a will is in place, resentments and feelings that the distribution is not equitable can further divide a family. When such problems arise during the course of family therapy, the therapist can help by providing a forum for the family members to air their differences. In addition, the therapist can structure a process for the family to resolve their resentments and feelings of unfairness.

---

* This problem is not specifically discussed in detail in this volume.

HE ALWAYS DID LIKE YOU BEST

FOR THE MEMBERS OF A FAMILY EXPERIENCING DISPUTES OR RESENTMENT OVER DISTRIBUTION OF A WILL

The following exercise will help each of you to identify your concerns regarding the distribution of an inheritance and express such concerns in a manner that other family members will be able to understand.

1. As a group, or individually, develop a list of reasons for how the deceased may have arrived at his or her decision to distribute assets in the manner that was executed.

2. When expressing your thoughts and feelings regarding the distribution, use "I" statements. These can be recorded, so as to use in a family session where you may feel more comfortable voicing such feelings.

3. Think about how each of your relatives may feel regarding the distribution. In the next family session, you should be prepared to acknowledge your perceptions of the feelings other members have.

4. Think about the pros and cons of rewriting a more equitable distribution of the inheritance (i.e., I want to maintain my relationship with a loved one).

5. Those family members interested and willing to redistribute his/her share of the inheritance should meet and discuss a more evenly distributed formula.

Section XXII

INTERRACIAL FAMILY PROBLEMS

THEY'RE CALLING ME A HALF-BREED

GOALS OF THE EXERCISE

1. Learn to cope effectively with the stress of being biracial.
2. Parents and children learn to support each other.

ADDITIONAL HOMEWORK THAT MAY BE APPLICABLE TO INTERRACIAL FAMILY PROBLEMS

ADDITIONAL PROBLEMS FOR WHICH THIS EXERCISE MAY BE USEFUL

• Jealousy

SUGGESTIONS FOR PROCESSING THIS EXERCISE WITH CLIENT

Interracial families frequently experience a variety of challenges and conflicts from within the family system as well as from society. These challenges and conflicts can involve the stress between parents who display some of their own hidden racial prejudices or from children who react in a resentful way toward their parents for their mixed race. Extended family members who disapprove of the interracial relationship can also create conflict and hardship. It is important that the therapist identify where these conflicts and challenges lie.

THEY'RE CALLING ME A HALF-BREED

FOR THE MEMBERS OF A FAMILY EXPERIENCING INTERRACIAL FAMILY PROBLEMS

This exercise will help you to express your thoughts and feelings about being a member of a biracial family. It will also help you as a family to increase your support for one another.

1. Over the next week each member is to identify times and the associated feelings when you have felt rejected or disapproved of for being part of a biracial family.

2. As a family get together before the next family session and describe these situations to each other.

3. Identify a list of people each of you feel is accepting and supportive. Before the next session, schedule at least one activity to complete with someone on your list.

4. As a family meet before the next family session and brainstorm the pros and cons of supporting one another and identifying social supports (e.g., extended family, friends in the community/church, coworkers).

Section XXIII

INTOLERANCE/DEFENSIVENESS

WHY CAN'T YOU UNDERSTAND MY SIDE FOR ONCE? (PART I)

GOALS OF THE EXERCISE

1. To reduce and possibly eliminate the tension and conflict regarding the attitudes of self-righteousness and superiority over others.
2. Become more open-minded and tolerant of one another.

ADDITIONAL HOMEWORK THAT MAY BE APPLICABLE TO INTOLERANCE/DEFENSIVENESS

ADDITIONAL PROBLEMS FOR WHICH THIS EXERCISE MAY BE USEFUL

- Anger
- Anxiety
- Depression

SUGGESTIONS FOR PROCESSING THIS EXERCISE WITH CLIENT

Attitudes of self-righteousness and superiority naturally create distance between individuals and can lead to resentment as well as end relationships. A family who is looking to prevent such consequences will need to identify the behaviors that family members engage in when these attitudes are evident. They will also need to identify the thoughts and feelings that these episodes instill. Additionally, all of this needs to be discussed as a family. It is important for family members to define what type of family life they want to have and what this would look like. Typically the first step in this process is helping the family members to identify and acknowledge each others' thoughts and feelings.

WHY CAN'T YOU UNDERSTAND MY SIDE FOR ONCE? (PART I)

FOR THE MEMBERS OF A FAMILY THAT IS EXPERIENCING INTERNAL PROBLEMS WITH INTOLERANCE AND DEFENSIVENESS

As a family agree on and commit to a time within the next week in which you can meet and complete the following activity:

1. Each family member is to identify a rather neutral issue and present his or her view of it. For example, one member can describe how he or she enjoys ice-skating.

2. Each family member is to then express agreement and understanding (regarding, for example, how his/her sibling or parent enjoys ice-skating).

3. The family should record or at least make a mental note of the following

    A. How she/he felt and thought when expressing his or her neutral issue.

    B. How she/he felt and thought when the others expressed acknowledgment and understanding.

    C. How she/he felt and thought when it was her or his turn to express acknowledgment and understanding.

WHY CAN'T YOU UNDERSTAND MY SIDE FOR ONCE? (PART II)

GOALS OF THE EXERCISE

1. Identify the roadblocks to talking without arguing.
2. Develop effective ways to talk with each other without arguing.

ADDITIONAL HOMEWORK THAT MAY BE APPLICABLE TO INTOLERANCE/DEFENSIVENESS

ADDITIONAL PROBLEMS IN WHICH THIS EXERCISE MAY BE USEFUL

- Anger
- Communication Problems

SUGGESTIONS FOR PROCESSING THIS EXERCISE WITH CLIENT

When family members cannot get their point across because of constant arguing, it is important to identify the process that is occurring (e.g., talking over each other, ignoring, etc.). In a session, the therapist can work with the family to identify these ineffective strategies and then to help implement signals or other ways to identify and interrupt this process. For example, when family members are talking over each other, assign a rule that the only one who can talk is the one with the "stress ball" in his/her hand. It may also be helpful to set a time limit (such as 1 or 2 minutes), after which the ball goes to another family member. This ball may also be substituted for a piece of linoleum, as in the exercise introduced by Markman, Stanley & Blumberg (1994) of "Who Has the Floor?" or the use of "Passing the hat" with families (Dattilio, 1994).

WHY CAN'T YOU UNDERSTAND MY SIDE FOR ONCE? (PART II)

This exercise should be attempted after you and your therapist have discussed and practiced strategies for managing conversations (i.e., stress ball to indicate who has the floor to speak) and deep breathing.

1. At home, family members can practice having conversations using the signals and strategies (i.e., stress ball) developed in the therapy session.

2. Family members should also practice deep breathing as a way to manage their feelings. You can visualize a thermometer, which will record the level of your feelings. When the thermometer is close to indicating a fever, practice deep breathing.

3. Sometimes when an individual cannot break his or her fever, a time-out is needed. When you need to take a time-out, try to set a time limit (such as 10 minutes). In using a time-out it is important that an attempt is made to continue the conversation. If this cannot be done, the topic should be discussed in the next session, where your therapist can help bring closure to the conversation.

JEALOUSY/INSECURITY

I AM NOT JEALOUS

GOALS OF THE EXERCISE

1. Reduce and/or eliminate feelings of jealousy/insecurity.
2. Eliminate blaming of each other regarding overt or perceived favoritism.

ADDITIONAL HOMEWORK THAT MAY BE APPLICABLE TO JEALOUSY/INSECURITY

ADDITIONAL PROBLEMS FOR WHICH THIS EXERCISE MAY BE USEFUL

- Anger Problems
- Anxiety
- Depression
- Selfishness*

SUGGESTIONS FOR PROCESSING THIS EXERCISE WITH CLIENT

Feelings of jealousy and insecurity can lead to very intense conflicts within family relationships. At times, a dependency ensues, leaving family members feeling trapped in a cycle. Other family members who observe the jealous and dependent behavior frequently become resentful and angry. Explain to family members their cycle and how destructive it can become. Once they have agreed to make some changes, provide them with the following exercise.

---

* This problem is not specifically discussed in detail in this volume.

I AM NOT JEALOUS

FOR THE MEMBERS OF A FAMILY THAT IS EXPERIENCING FEELINGS OF JEALOUSY/INSECURITY

Feelings of jealousy and insecurity can lead to very intense conflicts within family relationships. The following exercise is designed to help you reduce or eliminate feelings of jealousy/insecurity as well as blaming of each other regarding perceived or overt favoritism.

1. Identify what each of you believes to be the insecure and/or jealous behavior.

    I believe the jealous/insecure behavior is_____
    _____
    _____

    I believe the jealous/insecure behavior is_____
    _____
    _____

    I believe the jealous/insecure behavior is_____
    _____
    _____

    I believe the jealous/insecure behavior is_____
    _____
    _____

    I believe the jealous/insecure behavior is_____
    _____
    _____

    I believe the jealous/insecure behavior is_____
    _____
    _____

    I believe the jealous/insecure behavior is_____
    _____
    _____

I believe the jealous/insecure behavior is_____

_____

_____

2. Identify the thoughts that come to your mind when you observe these behaviors of jealousy.

When I see that jealous behavior I think _____

_____

When I see that jealous behavior I think _____

_____

When I see that jealous behavior I think _____

_____

When I see that jealous behavior I think _____

_____

When I see that jealous behavior I think _____

_____

When I see that jealous behavior I think _____

_____

3. Identify a list of alternative thoughts or actions, which can replace episodes of jealousy or insecurity. If you are having trouble, ask other family members for some input.

An alternative thought could be _____

_____

An alternative thought could be _____

_____

An alternative thought could be _____

_____

An alternative thought could be _____

_____

An alternative thought could be _____

_____

An alternative thought could be _____

_____

4. Practice taking a deep breath during situations in which you observe jealous/insecure behavior and think about the benefits of the alternative thoughts and/or actions.

Section XXV

LIFE-THREATENING/CHRONIC ILLNESS

JOHNNY HAS LEUKEMIA

GOALS OF THE EXERCISE

1. For family members to open up lines of communication regarding the terminal or chronic illness of one or more members.
2. To identify the primary areas of stress within the family and assess its effects.
3. To develop stress-reduction techniques and maintain or create a supportive family and social support network.

ADDITIONAL HOMEWORK THAT MAY BE APPLICABLE TO LIFE-THREATENING/CHRONIC ILLNESS

- Depression   What Do Others Value about Me?   Page 106
- Physical Disabilities   Why Is Dad in Bed All Day?   Page 180

ADDITIONAL PROBLEMS FOR WHICH THIS EXERCISE MAY BE USEFUL

- Family Conflicts*
- Physical Disabilities
- Single Parenting*

SUGGESTIONS FOR PROCESSING THIS EXERCISE WITH CLIENT

A life-threatening or chronic illness is often devastating, especially when it strikes a younger member or more than one member of the family. It is important for family members to be familiar with the various stages they will face with the progress of the illness (i.e., shock, denial, and grief). It is also important that family members identify and express the thoughts and feelings they are experiencing. Oftentimes it is helpful to identify a social support network. During the course of treatment, most families are dealing with issues such as stress, guilt, and depression regarding their son/daughter or parent or other relative who may be afflicted. The following exercise is designed to help families (including the member with the life-threatening chronic illness) to identify ways to reduce tension and stress.

---

* These problems are not specifically discussed in detail in this volume.

JOHNNY HAS LEUKEMIA

FOR THE MEMBERS OF A FAMILY EXPERIENCING A LIFE-THREATENING OR CHRONIC ILLNESS

The following exercise will help you as a family open up the lines of communication regarding the terminal or chronic illness. After completing the exercise, you should feel greater support from one another.

1. Each family member is to identify situations that create feelings of stress or conflict. Utilize "I" statements to facilitate a safe and nonthreatening atmosphere. For example, "I feel really stressed out when I have to cook dinner, clean up the dishes, and get ready to go visit Johnny in the hospital. I would feel calmer and would act more pleasant if everyone could pitch in and help."

2. Each family member is to identify what worries him/her the most about _____ chronic illness.

3. Each family member is to describe for the others the situations that create stress for him or her.

4. Each family member is to identify and express the positive feelings they have toward one another. The more reminders the better.

5. As a group, family members are to brainstorm ways in which they can reduce feelings of stress. To generate even more ideas, have them ask other family members or friends how they cope.

6. All family members need to stay in touch with their own level of stress (e.g., stress thermometer, or numerical rating 1 to 10) and identify at what level they need to practice deep breathing, taking a walk, working on a fun hobby/activity, asking for a hug, calling a friend, and so forth.

7. Community support groups that are comprised of other families with chronically ill members may also be something to try.

Section XXVI

MULTIPLE-BIRTH DILEMMAS

WITH SEVEN YOU GET AN EGGROLL

GOALS OF THE EXERCISE

1. Express thoughts and feelings regarding the birth of multiple children.
2. Identify stress management techniques to deal with the obligations and burdens of having multiple children.
3. Identify resources available and needed (physical, emotional, financial) to assist in childcare.

ADDITIONAL HOMEWORK THAT MAY BE APPLICABLE TO MULTIPLE-BIRTH DILEMMAS

- Anxiety   When I Feel Anxious It Is Like . . .   Page 32

ADDITIONAL PROBLEMS FOR WHICH THIS EXERCISE MAY BE USEFUL

- Unwanted/Unplanned Pregnancies

SUGGESTIONS FOR PROCESSING THIS EXERCISE WITH CLIENT

The birth of a child is a wondrous and miraculous event. Experiencing the birth of several at a time is even more miraculous but can be quite overwhelming as well. All members in the family will need to identify and express their feelings as the dichotomy of joy and stress abound.

WITH SEVEN YOU GET AN EGGROLL

FOR THE MEMBERS OF A FAMILY EXPERIENCING MULTIPLE BIRTHS

The birth of a child is a wondrous and miraculous event. Experiencing the birth of several at a time is even more miraculous but can be quite overwhelming as well. All members in the family will need to identify and express their feelings as the dichotomy of joy and stress abound.

1. Family members should first freely express their shock and fears with each other regarding being able to handle such responsibilities. (Try to use as many "I" statements as possible.)

2. As a group discuss various ways of handling stress. (Perhaps listing these ideas and putting the list where it can be easily accessed would be beneficial.) Typically with stress, individuals will engage in various types of negative self-talk. Such talk should be identified and replaced by positive and realistic statements.

3. Write a list of any negative statements. Additional statements can be added.

4. Write an alternative list that counters each negative statement. These two lists should be kept in plain view or easily accessible.

HOW ARE WE GOING TO DO THIS?

GOALS OF THE EXERCISE

1. To reduce the level of stress families will inevitably feel when experiencing simultaneous multiple births.
2. To identify ways of adjusting to the new family size and to the numerous responsibilities that accompany the births.

ADDITIONAL HOMEWORK THAT MAY BE APPLICABLE TO MULTIPLE-BIRTH DILEMMAS

*   Anxiety   When I Feel Anxious It Is Like . . .   Page 32

ADDITIONAL PROBLEMS FOR WHICH THIS EXERCISE MAY BE USEFUL

*   Unwanted/Unplanned Pregnancies

SUGGESTIONS FOR PROCESSING THIS EXERCISE WITH CLIENT

Families experiencing simultaneous multiple births will need to make many decisions regarding living arrangements, who can help and when, where will they get the clothes and food for their new babies, how will they pay for it all, and many others. Adjusting will require a significant amount of effort and energy as well as the support of others.

HOW ARE WE GOING TO DO THIS?

FOR THE MEMBERS OF A FAMILY EXPERIENCING MULTIPLE BIRTHS

It is tough enough for couples to have one child. The birth of multiple children increases such struggles and worries. This exercise will help you create some strategies for coping with the many stresses that accompany multiple childbirths.

1. Contact the nearest support group and attend two or three meetings.

2. Pull together other family members as well as friends who are willing to help out. Discuss what help is needed and at what times. Also, designate who in the family will coordinate these efforts.

3. Develop a daily schedule of who is doing what and when. Be sure that you include lighthearted family recreational activities at least every other week, or at least a weekly family meeting to discuss how each person is doing.

PERVASIVE DEVELOPMENTAL DISORDERS

KNOWING WHAT TO EXPECT

GOALS OF THE EXERCISE

1. To establish a daily routine for a child experiencing a pervasive developmental disorder.
2. To provide structure and security for the child.

ADDITIONAL HOMEWORK THAT MAY BE APPLICABLE TO PERVASIVE DEVELOPMENTAL DISORDER

- Behavioral Problems in Children   Charting Our Course   Page 48
  and Adolescents

ADDITIONAL PROBLEMS FOR WHICH THIS EXERCISE MAY BE USEFUL

- Mental Retardation*

SUGGESTIONS FOR PROCESSING THIS EXERCISE WITH CLIENT

Children with pervasive developmental disorders require a great deal of structure and consistency in their daily life. When change occurs (even in transitioning from one activity to another), problems of acting-out behavior such as yelling, screaming, and/or hitting can occur. In order to reduce the frequency of such behaviors, it is helpful to design a daily routine. It is also helpful to include visual aids so that the child can see himself/herself doing each activity.

---

* This problem is not specifically discussed in detail in this volume.

KNOWING WHAT TO EXPECT

FOR THE PARENTS OF A CHILD WITH A PERVASIVE DEVELOPMENTAL DISORDER

A child with a pervasive developmental disorder requires a great deal of structure and consistency in his/her daily life. When change occurs (even in transitioning from one activity to another), problems of acting-out behavior such as yelling, screaming, and/or hitting can occur. In order to reduce the frequency of such behaviors it is helpful to design a daily routine. It is also helpful to include visual aids so that your child can see himself or herself doing each activity. The following activity will help you get started toward creating a daily routine.

1. Make a chart identifying the activities your child generally engages in, and the corresponding times. For example:

	Monday
7:45	Wakes up
8:00	Gets dressed
8:15	Eats breakfast
8:45	Takes bus to school

2. Next to each activity and time, put a photograph of your child doing that activity. Or, have your child draw a picture of him or herself doing that activity.

Section XXVIII

PHYSICAL DISABILITIES

WHY IS DAD IN BED ALL DAY?

GOALS OF THE EXERCISE

1. For family members to open up lines of communication regarding the health problems affecting one of the members.
2. To prevent or reduce the distance as well as enmeshment that develops within family relationships.
3. Identify and express thoughts and feelings regarding the disability.

ADDITIONAL HOMEWORK THAT MAY BE APPLICABLE TO PHYSICAL DISABILITIES

*   Communication Problems   How Can I Talk So He'll Listen?   Page 87
*   Depression   What Do Others Value about Me?   Page 106
*   Life-Threatening/Chronic Illness   Johnny Has Leukemia   Page 169

ADDITIONAL PROBLEMS FOR WHICH THIS EXERCISE MAY BE USEFUL

*   Blended Families
*   Life-Threatening/Chronic Illnesses

SUGGESTIONS FOR PROCESSING THIS EXERCISE WITH CLIENT

Families who have a member with a chronic physical or mental disability oftentimes will experience a range of emotions such as confusion, anger, resentment, guilt, and/or sadness. Many times, family members prefer not to talk much about their feelings and thoughts regarding how the disabled member is affecting them. It is also typical for family members to not talk with the member who is disabled regarding such feelings. As a result, these thoughts and feelings remain tucked away, without much room for an outlet. In families who have a disabled member, it is important for a therapist to explore feelings.

In a family session the therapist should bring the topic of physical disabilities to light and process any fears or concerns with regard to discussing the issue. This may be difficult because it may be a family secret in the sense that "we don't talk about that topic." Once the therapist is able to get the family to a point of agreement that this topic needs to be discussed, suggest the following homework assignment.

WHY IS DAD IN BED ALL DAY?

FOR THE MEMBERS OF A FAMILY EXPERIENCING A DISABILITY

This exercise will help you as a family to open up the lines of communication regarding each others' thoughts and feelings about the disability.

1. Each family member is to think about and write down his/her own perceptions and understanding of what the disability involves (i.e., What is it called? How long will it last? Will it get any worse or better? What is the treatment for it?).

2. Identify the thoughts and feelings that each of you has when you think about the disability.

3. As a family, schedule a time to meet and discuss your responses to item 1. If this is too difficult, have the family members bring their responses and questions to the next counseling session to be processed with the therapist.

4. Schedule a weekly family meeting or activity to decrease any isolation of the family member with the disability and to reinforce a sense of family unity.

Section XXIX

RELIGIOUS/SPIRITUAL CONFLICTS

I DON'T KNOW WHAT TO BELIEVE IN ANYMORE

GOALS OF THE EXERCISE

1. Family members will be able to resolve interfaith conflicts.
2. Parents will be able to agree on child-rearing practices.

ADDITIONAL HOMEWORK THAT MAY BE APPLICABLE TO RELIGIOUS/SPIRITUAL CONFLICTS

ADDITIONAL PROBLEMS FOR WHICH THIS EXERCISE MAY BE USEFUL

Geographic Relocation

SUGGESTIONS FOR PROCESSING THIS EXERCISE WITH CLIENT

Religious conflicts often have a negative effect on child-rearing practices and can become a central point of contention within the marriage. As a result, children and adolescents will often reject both parents' religious faith/beliefs and refuse to participate in any services.

I DON'T KNOW WHAT TO BELIEVE IN ANYMORE

This exercise will help you in achieving some resolution to interfaith conflicts. You will need to meet as a family and be willing to listen to each other's comments and points of view.

1. As a family, construct a list of reasons to respect each person's religious faith/beliefs.

    I should respect _____ religious faith/beliefs because: _____

    _____

    _____

    _____

    _____

    _____

    _____

    _____

    _____

2. As a family, brainstorm a list of the pros and cons for continuing to be in conflict (Why we should continue to be conflicted? Why we should resolve this conflict?).

Continue in Conflict	Resolve the Conflict
_____	_____
_____	_____
_____	_____
_____	_____
_____	_____
_____	_____

3. Discuss the pros and cons of taking turns participating in both religions on a regular basis.

<table>
<tr><td align="center">Pros</td><td></td><td align="center">Cons</td></tr>
<tr><td>_____</td><td></td><td>_____</td></tr>
<tr><td>_____</td><td></td><td>_____</td></tr>
<tr><td>_____</td><td></td><td>_____</td></tr>
<tr><td>_____</td><td></td><td>_____</td></tr>
<tr><td>_____</td><td></td><td>_____</td></tr>
<tr><td>_____</td><td></td><td>_____</td></tr>
</table>

4. Each member could attend a service of the other's denomination in order to achieve a better understanding for each other's faith.

Section XXX

SCHIZOPHRENIA

MY BROTHER HEARS VOICES

GOALS OF THE EXERCISE

1. Identify thoughts and feelings regarding having a parent/spouse who hears voices.
2. Be able to express such thoughts and feelings.
3. For the family member experiencing the voices to express his/her thoughts and feelings.

ADDITIONAL HOMEWORK THAT MAY BE APPLICABLE TO SCHIZOPHRENIA

- Adoption
- Suicide Attempts

My Safe Place   Page 14
Creating a Positive Outlook   Page 204

ADDITIONAL PROBLEMS FOR WHICH THIS EXERCISE MAY BE USEFUL

- Anger
- Depression

SUGGESTIONS FOR PROCESSING THIS EXERCISE WITH CLIENT

Having a parent or family member who suffers from hallucinations can be very scary and confusing. Oftentimes this can be a family secret, which everyone knows about but never talks about. Even after a family is able to acknowledge that this is happening, talking about it can remain difficult. The following exercise is designed to assist family members in discussing their thoughts and feelings about this issue.

MY BROTHER HEARS VOICES

The following exercise will help you to discuss your thoughts and feelings regarding the family member who is hearing voices.

FOR THOSE WHO HAVE A SPOUSE OR FAMILY MEMBER WHO HEARS VOICES

1. Describe what your understanding is of someone who hears voices (describe what it might be like or why you think it happens). _____
   _____
   _____
   _____

2. When do you notice your _____ is hearing voices? How can you tell?
   _____
   _____
   _____

3. What do you do when your _____ is hearing voices? _____
   _____
   _____

4. What things do you worry about when your _____ is hearing voices?
   _____
   _____
   _____

5. What other thoughts and feelings do you have about your _____ hearing voices? _____
   _____
   _____

6. How would you like things to be different? _____

_____

_____

_____

FOR THE FAMILY MEMBER WHO IS HEARING THE VOICES

1. Describe what it is like for you when you are hearing voices? _____

_____

_____

_____

_____

2. What things do you worry about when you are hearing the voices? _____

_____

_____

_____

3. What other thoughts and feelings do you have about hearing the voices? _____

_____

_____

_____

_____

4. How does your family feel about you and about you hearing voices? _____

_____

_____

_____

_____

5. How do you feel about your family's feelings? _____

_____

_____

_____

_____

Section XXXI

SCHOOL PROBLEMS

MY TEENAGER IS TRUANT

GOALS OF THE EXERCISE

1. Parents vent their feelings of disappointment and frustration.
2. Parents verbalize the reasons for their expectations for son/daughter to succeed in school.
3. Parents identify their fears of son/daughter not succeeding in school.
4. Parents identify some of their own failed accomplishments that may be contributing to their frustration.
5. Identify triggers to wanting to avoid school or certain classes.
6. Identify alternative ways of coping by reviewing coping skills.
7. Increase the amount of time in school.

ADDITIONAL HOMEWORK THAT MAY BE APPLICABLE TO CLIENTS WITH TRUANCY PROBLEMS

ADDITIONAL PROBLEMS FOR WHICH THIS EXERCISE MAY BE USEFUL

*   Addictions
*   Oppositional Defiant Behavior*
*   Unwanted/Unplanned Pregnancy

SUGGESTIONS FOR PROCESSING THIS EXERCISE WITH CLIENT

This exercise is designed for students who are not attending classes or school on a regular basis. Meet with the student, parent(s), and school staff to gather relevant information regarding the duration that this behavior has been occurring and strategies already attempted. Chances are that the student is experiencing one of the following problems, which are interfering with his/her academic success: addiction, depression, anxiety, physical disability, and/or learning deficiency. Any of these issues that apply should be addressed in the current treatment plan.

---

* This problem is not specifically discussed in detail in this volume.

Parents should be given their assignment first. Once they complete the assignment, schedule a session to process their responses. This process should also be followed up with the student once he/she completes his/her assignment. Questions regarding substance use, depression, and anxiety should be posed during the sessions with parents and the student. Once these two sessions are completed, schedule a family session to discuss the results and impressions of the previous sessions.

MY TEENAGER IS TRUANT

FOR THE PARENTS

Please respond to the following questions before the next appointment.

A. What are my/our expectations of my/our son/daughter (e.g., I expect my son to maintain at least a "C" average and attend all classes on a daily basis)? Would I classify these expectations as realistic or unrealistic?

    1. _____

    2. _____

    3. _____

B. What may be some of the reasons for my/our son/daughter doing poorly in school? Here, parents should be encouraged to think in behavioral terms instead of personality traits (e.g., She does not do any homework, versus She is lazy). When these are discussed in a parent session, the possibility of substance use, depression, medical problems, learning difficulties, etc., should be considered.

    1. _____

    2. _____

    3. _____

C. What is your worst fear about your son/daughter not succeeding in school? Describe how it may have an impact on all members of the family. How will those who are important to you view you as a parent and as a person?

    1. _____

    2. _____

    3. _____

FOR THE STUDENT(S)

Please respond to the following questions before your next session.

A. What am I doing, as well as not doing, that may be causing me to do poorly in school?

   1. _____
   2. _____
   3. _____
   4. _____

B. How would my life be different if I were to improve my academic and behavioral performance?

   1. _____
   2. _____
   3. _____
   4. _____

C. What would I need to do in order to improve my performance in school (i.e., have more of a positive attitude, do more homework, decrease the amount of time that I spend fooling around)?

   1. _____
   2. _____
   3. _____
   4. _____

D. What would my life be like if I did not have to attend school?

   1. _____
   2. _____
   3. _____
   4. _____

E. If I truly do not care about school, then what are some of my alternatives?

   1. _____
   2. _____
   3. _____
   4. _____

F. How might my life be affected in the future if I were to fail out of school?

   1. _____
   2. _____
   3. _____

G. Why should I do better in school?

1. _____

2. _____

3. _____

Section XXXII

SEXUAL PREFERENCES

I AM STILL DANNY

GOALS OF THE EXERCISE

1. Family members discontinue blaming each other or resenting the family member who is gay.
2. Feelings of conflict and rejection are resolved and a plan of acceptance is embraced.
3. Family members develop a sense of understanding and acceptance for the family member's homosexuality.

ADDITIONAL HOMEWORK THAT MAY BE APPLICABLE TO SEXUAL PREFERENCES

- Anxiety   When I Feel Anxious It Is Like . . .   Page 32
- Communication Problems   How Can I Talk So He'll Listen?   Page 87
- Disillusionment with Family Ties   Circles of Perception   Page 112

ADDITIONAL PROBLEMS FOR WHICH THIS EXERCISE MAY BE USEFUL

- Blended Families
- Divorce
- Unwanted/Unplanned Pregnancies

SUGGESTIONS FOR PROCESSING THIS EXERCISE WITH CLIENT

The acceptance of alternative sexual lifestyles has been increasing over the years. Within some families, however, feelings of anger, resentment, and rejection remain strong. Such feelings arise for various reasons and could be explored within treatment sessions. Ultimately an individual needs to decide whether she/he will disclose this information to her/his family and friends (as well as which family members and which friends). Once the individual's orientation is disclosed, those made aware need to decide whether and to what degree they will accept that individual.

I AM STILL DANNY

1. An individual may be having difficulty deciding whether or not to tell his/her family about his/her sexual preference, or the family may be having difficulty accepting this news. Consequently, it is helpful to identify the fears each person has regarding such information (e.g., What will our friends think?). In addition to coping with fears, it is also important for individuals to identify the many other feelings that can become ignited regarding the issue of an alternative sexual lifestyle. Suggest to family members that they generate a list of the various fears as well as other feelings and thoughts. For example,

   When I heard the news I felt _____

   It made me think _____

2. All family members need to be able to express such feelings and their accompanying thoughts to one another. This can be done by writing a letter or by communicating in person. Before doing so, it might be beneficial for individuals to think about and practice what they want to say as well as what they expect to hear. To aid the process of acceptance, each family member should answer the questions associated with his/her fears and other thoughts and feelings. For example,

Questions / Fear / Feeling / Thought	*Response*
What if my friends think that I am gay or don't believe that I am not?	I know that I am not gay, besides, my true/close friends wouldn't care either way.

3. Sometimes individuals cannot approve of or agree with a family member's sexual choice. In order for a relationship to survive, there needs to be a sense of acceptance. Each of you needs to keep in mind your feelings for the member who is choosing an alternative sexual lifestyle. Describe/list the reasons you loved him/her before he/she expressed his/her sexual preference.

4. For the next week, focus only on the qualities beyond the sexuality of the family member. Focus on those qualities and how they may weigh against the issue of sexual preference.

Section XXXIII

SUICIDE ATTEMPTS

I WANT THINGS TO BE BETTER

GOALS OF THE EXERCISE

1. To reduce and eliminate thoughts and feelings about suicide or hurting oneself.
2. To instill a sense of hope in the person thinking about suicide.
3. To help the individual feeling/thinking this way to develop a better understanding as to how such thoughts and feelings develop.
4. To generate alternative plans to suicide or hurting oneself.

ADDITIONAL HOMEWORK THAT MAY BE APPLICABLE TO SUICIDE ATTEMPTS

• Adoption	My Safe Place	Page 14
• Child Sexual Abuse	A Picture Is Worth a Thousand Words (just pictures 1–3)	Page 81
• Depression	What Am I Thinking When I Am Feeling Depressed?	Page 104
• Depression	What Do Others Value about Me?	Page 106
• Suicide Attempts	Creating a Positive Outlook	Page 204

ADDITIONAL PROBLEMS IN WHICH THIS EXERCISE MAY BE USEFUL

*   Addictions
*   Anxiety
*   Depression
*   Family Conflict*

SUGGESTIONS FOR PROCESSING THIS EXERCISE WITH CLIENT

Many individuals thinking about suicide or wanting to hurt themselves feel that there is no hope of things changing. It is important to convey to these people that there are options and that things can get better. To do this it is also important for such individuals to become more aware of the triggers to such thoughts and feelings. The following exercise is designed to do this and to generate a prevention plan.

---

* This problem is not specifically discussed in detail in this volume.

I WANT THINGS TO BE BETTER

I am glad that you are taking the time to read this. That demonstrates that a part of you does want things to be better. Once you complete this exercise, you will have a plan of how you can take charge of making things better for you.

1. When you feel or think about suicide/hurting yourself, what has usually happened before you started thinking or feeling this way? _____

   _____

   _____

   _____

   _____

   _____

   _____

2. Describe the thoughts and feelings you experience during such times. _____

   _____

   _____

   _____

   _____

   _____

3. Where were you when you started to think/feel this way? _____

   _____

   _____

   _____

   _____

   _____

4. What did you do? _____

_____

_____

_____

_____

_____

5. How did you feel after you did this? _____

_____

_____

6. In what way was your behavior, as well as the thoughts and feelings you had, helpful?

_____

_____

_____

_____

_____

7. What is the negative side to such behavior, thoughts, and feelings?_____

_____

_____

_____

_____

_____

8. When else have you felt/thought this way but did not try to hurt yourself?_____

_____

_____

_____

9. What thoughts and/or behaviors stopped you from hurting yourself? _____

_____

_____

_____

_____

_____

10. What other things (people, activities, thoughts) have helped you to reduce the thoughts and/or feelings of wanting to hurt yourself? _____

_____
_____
_____
_____
_____

11. What else would help you to reduce such thoughts/feelings? _____

_____
_____
_____
_____
_____

12. Make a list of all the things that would help you reduce and possibly eliminate such thoughts and feelings (e.g., reminding yourself that this feeling will not last forever, spending time with a supportive friend or family member). _____

_____
_____
_____
_____
_____
_____

13. Describe how you would feel and what thoughts you would have while doing the things you just listed in item 12. _____

_____
_____
_____
_____
_____

CREATING A POSITIVE OUTLOOK

GOALS OF THE EXERCISE

1. To generate a sense of hope.
2. To identify the positives in one's life (or, reasons for living).
3. To recognize who the support people are in your life.

ADDITIONAL HOMEWORK THAT MAY BE APPLICABLE TO SUICIDE ATTEMPTS

•	Addictions	Staying Clean	Page 2
•	Addictions	What Else Can I Do?	Page 5
•	Adoption	My Safe Place	Page 14
•	Child Sexual Abuse	A Picture Is Worth a Thousand Words (just pictures 1–3)	Page 81
•	Depression	What Am I Thinking When I Am Feeling Depressed?	Page 104
•	Depression	What Do Others Value about Me?	Page 106

ADDITIONAL PROBLEMS FOR WHICH THIS EXERCISE MAY BE USEFUL

• Depression
• Family Conflict*

SUGGESTIONS FOR PROCESSING THIS EXERCISE WITH CLIENT

Individuals experiencing thoughts and feelings about suicide or a wish to harm oneself need to develop a sense of optimism and positiveness in their lives. They need to focus in on the things in their lives that are and have been good. These can involve memories of good times they've shared with others, times they accomplished something positive or worthwhile, or times when they received something they really wanted. Encouraging individuals to focus on identifying such thoughts and feelings gives credence to the belief that life can be good and has not been ALL bad.

---

* This problem is not specifically discussed in detail in this volume.

CREATING A POSITIVE OUTLOOK

You are now on your way to making things better for yourself. After completing this exercise, you will have created a more positive outlook for yourself and your future.

1. Describe a time you laughed really hard. _____
    _____
    _____
    _____
    _____
    _____
    _____

2. Describe a time you completed something well (i.e., got a high mark on a test, scored a point in a game, received a compliment). _____
    _____
    _____
    _____
    _____
    _____
    _____

3. Identify and describe two or three people who make you feel good. _____
    _____
    _____
    _____
    _____
    _____

4. Identify and describe at least three things that you do that make you feel good._____

    _____

    _____

    _____

    _____

    _____

5. In the next week schedule a time when you will do at least two of the things that you listed in item 4. _____

    Time

    Sunday   _____

    Monday   _____

    Tuesday   _____

    Wednesday   _____

    Thursday   _____

    Friday   _____

    Saturday   _____

6. Describe a plan of how you will spend more time with the people you identified in item 3 and how you can do what you identified in item 5 more often._____

    _____

    _____

    _____

    _____

UNWANTED/UNPLANNED PREGNANCIES

HONEY, GUESS WHAT?

GOALS OF THE EXERCISE

1.   Unite/reunite family relationships by being able to express individual thoughts and feelings about the unplanned pregnancy.
2.   Identify and demonstrate ways of being supportive to one another (especially the individual who is pregnant).
3.   Formulate a plan of what to do (i.e., having the child and deciding how to raise him/her, pursuing adoption, or other alternatives).

ADDITIONAL HOMEWORK THAT MAY BE APPLICABLE TO UNWANTED/UNPLANNED PREGNANCIES

*   Geographic Relocation   Should We or Should We Not?   Page 150

ADDITIONAL PROBLEMS FOR WHICH THIS EXERCISE MAY BE USEFUL

*   Multiple-Birth Dilemmas

SUGGESTIONS FOR PROCESSING THIS EXERCISE WITH CLIENT

An unplanned pregnancy can be both a joyous surprise and a scary and gut-wrenching dilemma. When an unexpected pregnancy emerges within couple or family treatment, the decision of what to do can be overwhelmingly difficult to determine. Regardless of the decision, support and communication regarding the various feelings and thoughts that arise is essential. The following homework is a guideline for how to process such a dilemma.

HONEY, GUESS WHAT?

Support and communication regarding the various thoughts and feelings that one has about pregnancy are always essential. The following homework exercise is a guideline for how you can maintain/create the support you need at this particular time. In completing it, you will also open up the lines of communication, in order to express the various thoughts and feelings and needs that each of you have regarding your pregnancy.

1. Each family member is to identify the various thoughts and feelings he/she has regarding the pregnancy. Record these on paper.

2. Remember to use "I" statements and to refrain from any blaming or derogatory remarks.

3. Schedule a family meeting, and have each member share his/her thoughts and feelings. If this creates chaos, have a family session so that your therapist can facilitate the process.

Once you have completed the above, proceed to the next step.

4. Throughout the next week, each family member is to imagine having a baby in the home. Family members can talk to others (family, friends, or a support group) regarding how things will be different once a baby arrives, and how each person and the family as a whole will be affected.

Once you have completed this, try the next step.

5. Brainstorm a list of the pros and cons for all options considered.

Option	Pros	Cons
_____	_____	_____
_____	_____	_____
_____	_____	_____
_____	_____	_____
_____	_____	_____

6. Decide on an option and describe who will do what. _____

   _____

   _____

   _____

   _____

7. Identify individuals who are considered supportive to the person who is pregnant and to other family members who are affected and involved. My support people are

   _____

   _____

8. Have each member describe ways he/she wants support, reassurance, comfort, and so forth regarding the decision made. _____

   _____

   _____

   _____

   _____

   _____

BIBLIOGRAPHY

Bonkowski, S. (1990a). *Children Are Nondivorceable.* Chicago: ACTA Publications.

Bonkowski, S. (1990b). *Teens Are Nondivorceable.* Chicago: ACTA Publications.

Brown, L.K., and M. Brown. (1998). *Dinosaurs Divorce: A Guide for Changing Families.* New York: DEMCO Media.

Dattilio, F.M. (2000). "Graphic Perceptions." In R.E. Watts (ed.) *Techniques in Marriage and Family Counseling,* Vol. 1 (45–51). Alexandria, Virginia: American Counseling Association.

Dattilio, F.M. (1994). "Families in crisis." In F.M Dattilio and A. Freeman (eds.) *Cognitive-Behavioral Strategies in Crisis Intervention* (278–301). New York: Guilford.

Dattilio, F.M. (1997). "Family Therapy." In R. Leahy (ed.) *Practicing Cognitive Therapy: A Guide to Interventions* (409–450). Northvale, New Jersey: Jason Aronson, Inc.

Dattilio, F.M. (2001). "Cognitive-Behavior Family Therapy: Contemporary Myths and Common Misperceptions." *Contemporary Family Therapy: An International Journal* 23:1 (39–52).

Dattilio, F.M., N.B. Epstein, and D.H. Baucom. (1998). "An Introduction to Cognitive-Behavior Therapy with Couples and Families" (1–36). In F.M. Dattilio (ed.) *Case Studies in Couple and Family Therapy: Systemic and Cognitive Perspectives.* New York: Guilford.

Dattilio, F.M. and A.E. Jongsma. (2000). *The Family Therapy Treatment Planner.* New York: John Wiley & Sons, Inc.

Markman, H.J., S. Stanley, and S.L. Blumberg. (1994). *Fighting for Your Marriage.* San Francisco: Jossey-Bass.

Weeks, G.R. and S. Treat. (1992). *Couples In Treatment: Techniques for Effective Practices.* New York: Brunner/Mazel.

ABOUT THE AUTHORS

Louis J. Bevilacqua, Psy.D. is the Clinical Director of Connections Adolescents and Family Care, a private psychotherapy practice in Exton, Pennsylvania. He is a National Board Certified Counselor and coeditor of the book *Comparative Treatments for Relationship Dysfunction* (2000).

Frank M. Dattilio, Ph.D., ABPP holds joint affiliations in psychiatry at the University of Pennsylvania School of Medicine and Harvard Medical School. He is a Clinical Psychologist, Clinical Member, and Approved Supervisor of AAMFT. He is also the author of more than 120 professional books and journal articles and is a noted lecturer worldwide.

ABOUT THE DISK

INTRODUCTION

The forms on the enclosed disk are saved in Microsoft Word for Windows version 7.0. In order to use the forms, you will need to have word processing software capable of reading Microsoft Word for Windows version 7.0 files.

SYSTEM REQUIREMENTS

- IBM PC or compatible computer
- 3.5″ floppy disk drive
- Windows 95 or later
- Microsoft Word for Windows version 7.0 (including the Microsoft converter*) or later or other word processing software capable of reading Microsoft Word for Windows 7.0 files.

  *Word 7.0 needs the Microsoft converter file installed in order to view and edit all enclosed files. If you have trouble viewing the files, download the free converter from the Microsoft web site. The URL for the converter is:
  http://officeupdate.microsoft.com/downloadDetails/wd97cnv.htm

  Microsoft also has a viewer that can be downloaded, which allows you to view, but not edit documents. This viewer can be downloaded at:
  http://officeupdate.microsoft.com/downloadDetails/wd97vwr32.htm

Note: Many popular word processing programs are capable of reading Microsoft Word for Windows 7.0 files. However, users should be aware that a slight amount of formatting might be lost when using a program other than Microsoft Word. If your word processor cannot read Microsoft Word for Windows 7.0 files, unformatted text files have been provided in the TXT directory on the floppy disk.

HOW TO INSTALL THE FILES ONTO YOUR COMPUTER

To install the files follow these instructions:

1. Insert the enclosed disk into the floppy disk drive of your computer.
2. From the Start Menu, choose **Run**.
3. Type **A:\SETUP** and press **OK**.

4. The opening screen of the installation program will appear. Press **OK** to continue.

5. The default destination directory is `C:\Family`. If you wish to change the default destination, you may do so now.

6. Press **OK** to continue. The installation program will copy all files to your hard drive in the `C:\Family` or user-designated directory.

USING THE FILES

Loading Files

To use the word processing files, launch your word processing program. Select **File, Open** from the pull-down menu. Select the appropriate drive and directory. If you installed the files to the default directory, the files will be located in the `C:\Family` directory. A list of files should appear. If you do not see a list of files in the directory, you need to select **WORD DOCUMENT (*.DOC)** under **Files of Type**. Double-click on the file you want to open. Edit the file according to your needs.

Printing Files

If you want to print the files, select **File, Print** from the pull-down menu.

Saving Files

When you have finished editing a file, you should save it under a new file name by selecting **File, Save As** from the pull-down menu.

USER ASSISTANCE

If you need assistance with installation or if you have a damaged disk, please contact Wiley Technical Support at:

Phone: (212) 850-6753

Fax: (212) 850-6800 (Attention: Wiley Technical Support)

E-mail: techhelp@wiley.com

To place additional orders or to request information about other Wiley products, please call (800) 225-5945.

For information about the disk see pages 215–216.

WILEY
Publishers Since 1807

DATE DUE